Before You Buy

An Engagement Ring

Nancy N. Schiffer

With A 4-Step Guide For Making The Right Choice

Schiffer ®
Publishing Ltd

4880 Lower Valley Road, Atglen, PA 19310 USA

Title page: Modern rings designed by Bagley & Hotchkiss. *Courtesy of www.weddingband.com.*

Contents page: Platinum and 18K gold engagement ring designed by Judith Evans. *Courtesy of www.weddingband.com.* Mounting only: $900.

Schiffer, Nancy N.
  Before you buy an engagement ring / Nancy N. Schiffer.
    p.   cm.
    Includes bibliographical references and index.
    ISBN 0-7643-0611-1
    1. Diamonds--Purchasing 2. Rings--Purchasing 3. Gems--Purchasing. I. Title II. Title: Engagement Ring.
TS753.S38   1999
736'.23'0297--dc21   98-40836
                                              CIP

Book design by Blair Loughrey
Typeset in Dutch 801 / Zapf Humanist

ISBN: 0-7643-0611-1
Printed in China
1 2 3 4

Published by Schiffer Publishing Ltd.
4880 Lower Valley Road
Atglen, PA 19310
Phone: (610) 593-1777; Fax: (610) 593-2002
E-mail: Schifferbk@aol.com
Please visit our web site catalog at **WWW.Schifferbooks.com**

This book may be purchased from the publisher.
Include $3.95 for shipping.
Please try your bookstore first.
We are interested in hearing from authors
with book ideas on related subjects.
You may write for a free catalog.

Contents

ACKNOWLEDGMENTS   4
INTRODUCTION   5
   Antique Rings   6
   Traditions   6
1 DIAMONDS   10
   Where Diamonds Come From   10
   The Four "C"s   15
      Cut and Proportion   15
      Color   34
      Clarity and Perfection   37
      Carat Weight   40
   Diamond Grading Reports   42
   Identification Systems   44
   Diamond Imitations   45
2 COLORED STONES AND PEARLS   46
   Color Groups   48
   Emerald   50
   Ruby   51
   Sapphire   52
   Pearl   56
3 YOUR SETTING   59
   Metals   59
      Gold   59
      Platinum   63
   Silver & Other Metals   66
   Setting Styles   67
   Custom Designing Your Engagement Ring   83
   Ring Sets and Wedding Bands   84
4 AFTER YOU CHOOSE YOUR ENGAGEMENT RING   94
   Written Guarantees   94
   Paying for the Ring   97
   Insurance   97
   Care of Your Ring   97
5 A 4-STEP GUIDE TO MAKING THE RIGHT CHOICE   99
BIBLIOGRAPHY   102
INDEX   102

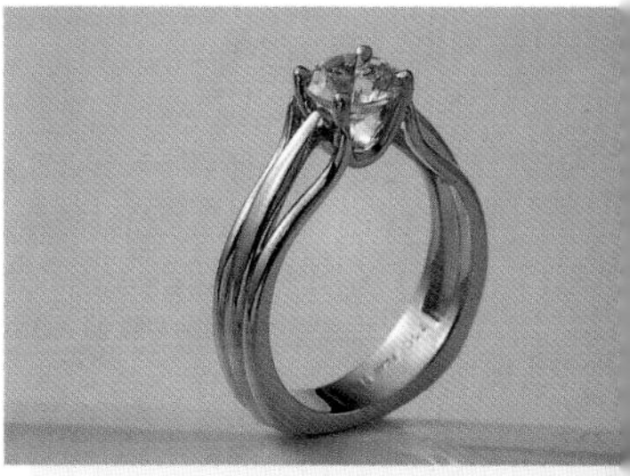

Acknowledgments

Many people have contributed information and photographs to this book. I sincerely thank: Sonya and David Newell-Smith at Tadema Gallery in London; Joan Munves Boening at James Robinson, Inc. in New York; Jason Robbins at Leo Robbins & Sons, Inc. in Philadelphia and Robbins Online Jewelry Store at www.weddingband.com or contact Jason Robbins at 1-800-777-4452 x151; Robin Walker and J. N. Evans Lombe at Central Selling Organisation in London; Lisa Caceci at Diamond Information Center in New York; and Bruce M. Waters at the photo studio and back cover bottom photograph. May this book bring you benefits forever.

Left: Lady's 14K gold and diamond mounting with 8 baguettes and 8 marquise stones of 1.40 ct total weight designed by Martin Flyer. *Courtesy of www.weddingband.com.* Mounting only: $3,000.

Right: Lady's 18K yellow gold, platinum, and diamond mounting designed by Mark Michael Designs. *Courtesy of www.weddingband.com.*

Introduction

Suddenly, you are engaged! Congratulations and much happiness to you.

This book can help you choose the ring to symbolize your new status and intention to be married. Your ring will announce to all who see it that you are about to accept an important role in your society by pledging yourself to the responsibilities of marriage. Your ring will also say something about you.

The more you know about the interesting terms, materials, and significances that make up your ring, the more confidence you will have in it. Your ring can reflect your individuality. To be a smart and interested shopper, you may need a little information to build on. Asking the right questions will enable you to be the educated consumer and this book is designed to help you achieve that goal.

10X Magnification

The features of an engagement ring (and other jewelry) that affect the value and the grading of stones are those that can be seen at 10X magnification, a standard throughout the jewelry industry. The naked eye probably will not pick up the individual features. Those features that cannot be seen at 10X magnification are considered not to exist. A small tool to aide you is a 10X magnifier known as a "**loupe**," which all jewelry stores will have available for your use; one also can easily be obtained from an optical supply business.

Antique Rings

Before you choose a ring, you may want to consider the benefits and feelings that an older or antique ring would give you. There are many fine antique rings available in a variety of materials and price ranges.

The purchase of an antique ring as your engagement ring may be appealing to couples for many reasons. First or subsequent marriages may be signified by choosing rings with a past. The continuity implied by a ring that belonged to a special person can be powerful. Older rings can be of a preferred style and quality that is hard to find on the "new" market. Family sentiment and tradition may indicate that an older style is appropriate and desirable for the new couple.

Traditions

An Egyptian scarab dating between 1900 and 1550 B.C. depicts in hieroglyphics the hopeful message "every good thing" (Chadour, vol 1, p. 3). And since at least the early second century, pictorial representations of people wearing more than one finger ring remain (Ibid., p. xix). Literary sources also record finger rings among the ancients. In the succeeding centuries, artists have depicted finger rings on all manner of royal and lowly people. Rings have represented high offices, beauty, and wealth as well as memberships in organizations, gifts of great merit, and roles in society.

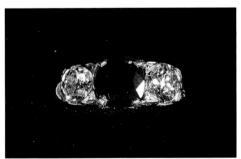

Left: American platinum, sapphire, and diamond three-stone ring, c.1920. *Courtesy James Robinson, NY, NY.* $42,500 - 51,000.

Below: **Engraving on the shank** is typical of the style popular in the 1920s. American platinum and diamond ring with built-up openwork setting with millegraining, center diamond approx. 2.6 ct and small diamonds with engraving on the shank, c.1920. *Courtesy James Robinson, NY, NY.* $48,500 - 58,200.

6

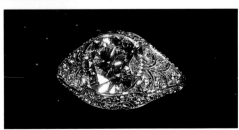

The custom of giving an engagement ring to announce pending betrothal was established for European royalty in the sixteenth century. Gradually, as the merchant class in England acquired wealth and jewelry, the tradition of an engagement ring grew more widespread. Growing populations carried forth their cultures into new places and whole industries developed to serve their desires. The sense of jewelry's significance and beauty is no different today.

Ring in gold with opal designed by Archibald Knox for Liberty & Co., London, c.1905. *Courtesy of Tadema Gallery, London.*

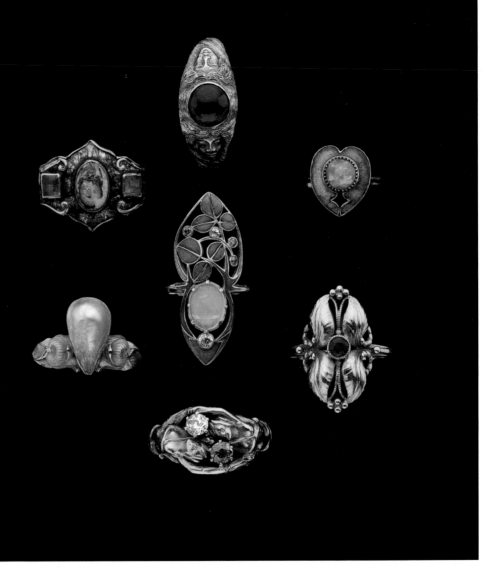

Seven Art Nouveau rings made c.1900. Top: by an unknown maker. Second row: three stones and enamel by James Cromar Watt, one stone and enamel by Child & Child. Center: opal and diamonds by Georges le Turcq. Fourth row: pearl and enamel attributed to Beaudouin, single stone and gold leaves by Evald Nielsen. Bottom: two stones and gold torsos by Maison Vever, c.1890. *Courtesy of Tadema Gallery, London.*

Seven Arts and Crafts rings by British designers, c.1900 to 1915. Top: with pearl and triangular colored stone, not attributed. Second row: with pearls by Edward Spencer, with emeralds by Henry Wilson. Center: by Arthur and Georgie Gaskin. Fourth row: turquoise by Ella Naper, colored stone by Henry Wilson. Bottom: four opals by John Paul Cooper. *Courtesy of Tadema Gallery, London.*

George III 18K gold and stone cameo of Socrates, English, c.1790. *Courtesy James Robinson, NY, NY.* $3,750 - 4,500.

1 *Diamonds*

The Centenary Diamond found at the Premier Mine in South Africa on July 17, 1986. It weighed 599 carats rough and was cut to a finished wieght of 273.85 carats with 247 facets. DeBeers Consolidated Mines celebrated its 100th year in 1988 by naming it the Centenary. *Courtesy Diamond Information Center.*

In the twentieth century, gem-quality diamonds are practically a global symbol of love. Once, ownership was reserved for royal families who could afford the high cost of diamonds, the rare and splendid fruits of nature. However, during the nineteenth century, vast mining operations in South Africa (See the following section "Where Diamonds Come From.") brought the diamond market down to a level where more people could afford them.

Diamonds are the hardest natural substance known. Composed of pure, crystallized carbon, diamonds are the simplest of all gems in terms of their chemistry. Only about twenty percent of the diamonds mined are of gem quality. The vast majority of diamonds are opaque and used in industrial applications. Although white diamonds are best known in the jewelry trade, fancy colored diamonds are also found with varying frequency in different parts of the world. (See the section below on diamond "Color"). When cut in facets with particular geometric proportions, diamonds refract light into a brilliant display. These characteristics have given diamonds the reputation for endurance and excitement: two cherished attributes of love.

Diamond Traditions

Diamond is the birthstone of April (along with sapphire) and the special stone of Friday.

Ancient astrologers designated diamonds as powerful for people governed by Mars. Diamonds were credited with providing fortitude, love in marriage, and protection from witchcraft, poisons, and nightmares.

The symbolism of diamonds as a love token has been encouraged by the world diamond industry throughout the twentieth century. The cultivation of this industry has grown and become refined into one of the most well-organized businesses in the world. Competition among dealers today stimulates the market and breeds high standards of quality and value.

Where Diamonds Come From

The Jwaneng open pit mine in Africa. © DeBeers.

Diamonds on the market today have a fascinating history. The conditions that produce diamonds are scarce, and so diamonds are a rare product of natural phenomena. They were created in **volcanic pipes** from the molten center of the earth. Over millions of years, if all the heat, pressure, and chemical components are right, such pipes produce occasional diamonds. When cooled, pure carbon molecules subjected to intense heat and pressure crystallize into diamonds. The volcanic pipes that have produced diamonds are widely scattered across the world.

11

Coastal mining in Africa. © DeBeers.

Man has gathered diamonds from **alluvial deposits** in river beds and streams since the earliest times. Ancient diamonds were found in India from the riverbeds and on the west coast of Africa, in the area known as the Diamond Coast. Alluvial diamonds have washed down from their sources thousands of miles upstream over thousands of years and have become imbedded deep in the lighter sand along the coast and the heavy gravel above bedrock. To uncover these diamonds today, miners must dig down 70 feet or more through sand to reach the level where the diamonds rest. For every carat of rough diamond uncovered, 28 tons of sand and gravel on average must be dug. And only a small percent of the rough can be used in jewelry.

When a rare source of diamonds is located, **diamond mines** are dug to recover the diamonds. It is rare that a diamond mine bears sufficient high quality stones to make the project practical. Before the 18th century, India had the only known diamond mines, but in about 1730, major deposits were found in Brazil. Other deposits of gem-quality diamonds were found in 1867 in South Africa, in 1957 in Siberia, and in 1979 in Australia. Current explorations for diamond-bearing volcanic pipes elsewhere, particularly in China, Canada, and the United States, have brought hope that these and other areas too, may also produce significant quantities of gem-quality diamonds in the future.

Top: The Kimberley Mine in South Africa in the early days, c.1872-73. © DeBeers.

Above: Underground drilling for diamonds at the Finsch Mine in South Aftica. © DeBeers.

Left: The big hole at Kimberley Mine as seen today with the town of Kimberley, South Africa, at the top.

13

Diamonds of gem quality are only a small percent of what is uncovered from the world's diamond mines and alluvial deposits. Diamonds of lesser quality for industrial use are very important to the diamond industry and world economy. Today, about one third of the current new production of industrial diamonds come from Australia, with the other areas ranked in descending order as follows: Zaire, Botswana, Siberia, South Africa, and the rest of the world.

Once gem-quality diamond crystals are found, mined, and sorted by weight, color, and clarity, they are studied and cut into the most suitable shape and size for each diamond. Today, major diamond cutting centers are in India, Israel, Antwerp, and New York.

Left: Cutting diamonds. © DeBeers.

Right: Cutting and polishing a diamond. *Courtesy Diamond Information Center.*

Above: Holding two diamonds. *Courtesy Diamond Information Center.*

Left: Sorting diamonds. © DeBeers.

14

Today, the monetary value of a diamond depends on a combination of four variable attributes: **cut, color, clarity**, and **carat** weight. Each of these attributes, known as "the four Cs," have many variations, which are explained below. It is up to the customer to choose the combination of these variables that best fit their needs.

When the grade of color is considered along with each degree of perfection and each shading of quality in cutting, literally hundreds of possible combinations arise that can affect the value of a diamond at any given weight – which is why a diamond expert can only smile and sadly shake his head when someone asks him what a one-carat diamond is worth. The only way to receive a more accurate reply is to ask: "Which one-carat diamond are you speaking of?"

Cut and Proportion

Cut and proportion in diamonds is the only variable that man has a hand in: The other three are present in nature, without our help. In their natural state, diamond crystals are shaped as a double pyramid. They are cut and polished to a shape that will best enable the diamond to break up light into a prism of rainbow colors. To chose the cut, a diamond is studied to determine its optimal final shape. The monetary values of two diamonds of the same color, clarity, and weight can differ dramatically due to differences in the quality of their cutting and in their proportion.

The cut and proportion of a diamond has the most influence on the **brilliance** of the stone. Poorly cut or poorly proportioned diamonds look dull, not fiery and full of light as you would like them to look. Gem-quality diamonds may loose more than half their original weight when they are cut from the original crystals.

The rough diamond is usually shaped as an octahedron, that is, two four-sided pyramids joined at their bases. The first step in cutting is to divide the diamond into two parts, by sawing it a little above the middle. The rough diamond is then put into a clamp and brought down into the edge of a phosphor-bronze blade revolving at high speed. The edge of the blade is kept coated with diamond dust, because only a diamond can cut a diamond. The larger piece of the rough stone is mounted into a lathe and turned at high speed while another diamond is held against it. This process is called rounding or girdling, because it changes the four-sided crystal into a round one.

15

Next, the facets are cut precisely around the diamond. Eight main facets are ground into the diamond above the girdle and eight main facets below the girdle.

The rest of the facets are cut by dividing up the main facets, as shown in the diagram

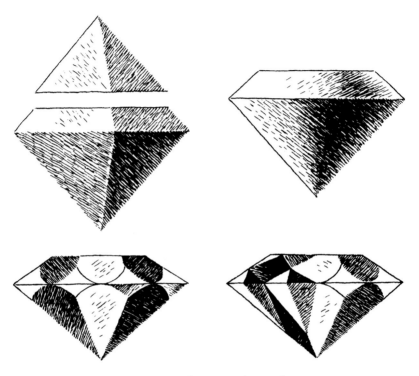

Four stages of cutting a diamond.

Make

The overall brilliance and value of a diamond is determined by the **make** of the diamond. The "make" reflects how well the stone is cut, its proportions, and the precision with which the facets are placed; in other words, whether it is "well made." Diamonds of comparable color, clarity, and weight may actually differ in overall quality and, thus, value, because the characteristics of their cuts are different; these characteristics determine the "make."

Today, round diamonds are usually full-cut with 58 facets: 1 as the table, 33 on the crown, and 24 on the pavilion; this is called the **brilliant cut**. In addition to being symmetrical, the facets must be placed at very exact angles.

In a **round** cut diamond, which is the most common cut, the following diagram shows the names of the parts of the stone.

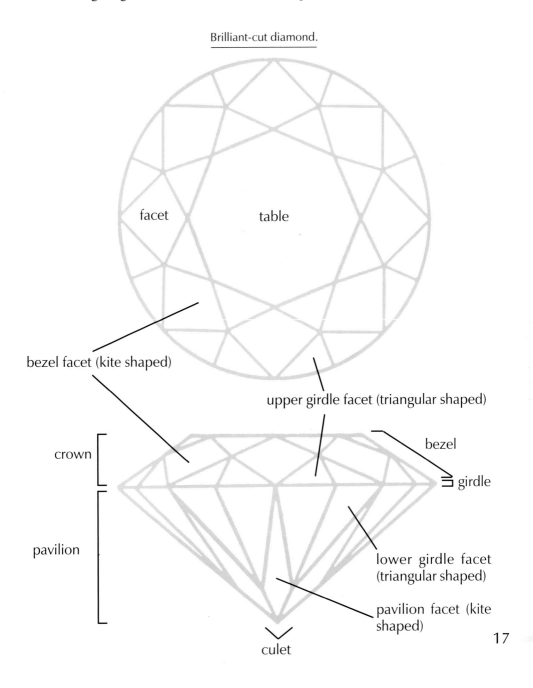

Brilliant-cut diamond.

facet

table

bezel facet (kite shaped)

upper girdle facet (triangular shaped)

bezel

girdle

crown

pavilion

lower girdle facet (triangular shaped)

pavilion facet (kite shaped)

culet

17

Faulty cuts on diamonds.

Off-center culet

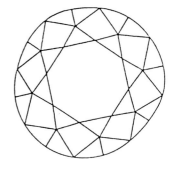

Slightly out-of-round girdle outline

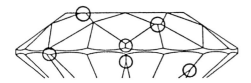

facets are not pointed properly

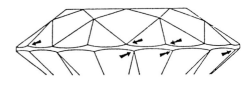

Crown and pavilion misalignment

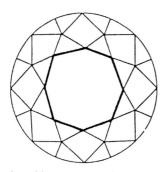

The table is not a regular octagon

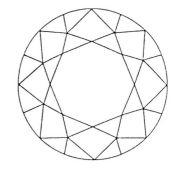

Misshapen facets

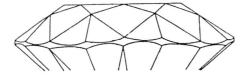

Wavy girdle

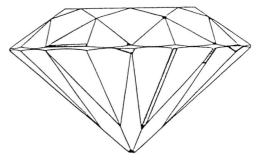

Extra facets

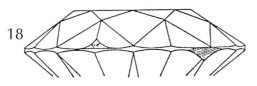

Natural flaws on the crown and pavilion

The brilliance of the diamond depends on the angles of the facets to each other and their relative size. Modern cutting is based on a knowledge of how the diamond refracts light. You want the maximum amount of the light that enters the diamond to be refracted back through the top.

Faulty cuts such as **sloping table facets**, a **chipped** or **off-center culet**, and **poor symmetry** can diminish the value of an otherwise good quality diamond. **Wavy** and **rough girdles** are also bad features of a cutting and will diminish the value of a diamond.

Older stones were cut in various shapes according to the technology and preferences of the time. In the 16th century, **table cut** diamonds were flat and **rose cut** diamonds had a flat base with six radiating facets in round, pear, and oval shapes. The **old-mine cut** was a cushion shape with more than 58 facets, a high crown, and deep pavilion, just barely rounded off from the diamond crystal shape. Similar to the old mine cut but more rounded, the **European cut** was especially popular around 1850 with 58 facets on a round diamond with a high crown and deep pavilion.

You may have heard that your great-grandmother's **old mine cut** or old **European cut** diamond are not as valuable as diamonds today. That is true. When your great-grandmother's diamond was cut, jewelers did not have the knowledge that we have today about what a diamond does with light, so they cut the diamond to preserve as much weight as possible. Old mine and European cut diamonds are generally **deep cut** stones where light that enters the top of the stone can escape through the side. Unfortunately, maximum brilliance is not achieved.

A good cut provides maximum light reflection back through the table.

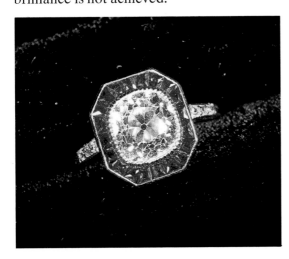

Old mine cut diamond. Continental 18 K gold and platinum ring with an old mine cut diamond of approximately 2.1 ct in bezel setting with millegraine edge, and rubies, c.1900. *Courtesy James Robinson, NY, NY.* $23,500 - 28,200.

19

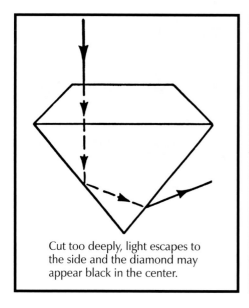

Cut too deeply, light escapes to the side and the diamond may appear black in the center.

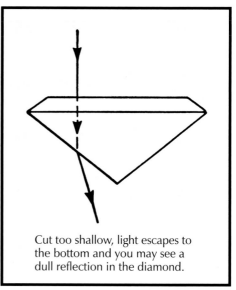

Cut too shallow, light escapes to the bottom and you may see a dull reflection in the diamond.

There are also old diamonds that are cut too shallow where light that enters the top of the stone can escape through the bottom. These are called **swindled** stones. Again, maximum brilliance is not achieved.

If you have an old diamond of good quality, you might consider having it re-cut. Although it will weigh less than it did before, it will often look larger because the re-cutting causes it to be much more brilliant. The cost for re-cutting an old diamond is usually about $150-200 per carat, far less than the cost of a new stone. For sentimental reasons, some people like to leave old stones in their original settings. However, old stones can appear beautifully in new settings, which can also give a different personality to the ring.

Over time and through experience, the best proportions to maximize the reflective brilliance of round diamonds (their fire) have developed. In determining the best proportion of a diamond, a few different theories exist. For the most part, however, all fall into a narrow range, generally agreeing that the crown height should be about 1/3 the height of the pavilion.

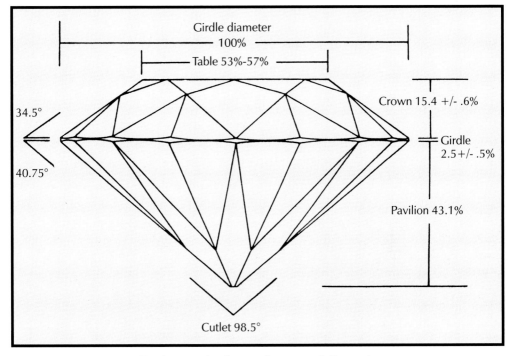

Girdle diameter
100%

Table 53%-57%

34.5°

Crown 15.4 +/- .6%

Girdle
2.5 +/- .5%

40.75°

Pavilion 43.1%

Cutlet 98.5°

Good proportion for a well-cut round diamond.

Brilliant-cut
round diamond.
*Courtesy
Diamond
Information
Center.*

21

Platinum and diamond mounting with 40 **brilliants** of 0.25 ct total weight designed by Infinity Line. *Courtesy of www.weddingband.com.* Mounting only: $1,200.

Lady's 18K gold and diamond mounting with 2 **brilliants** of .06 ct total weight designed by J. A. Bevacqua. *Courtesy of www.weddingband.com.* Mounting only: $900.

Lady's 18K gold and diamond mounting with 4 **brilliants** of 0.17 tw designed by J. A. Bevaqua. *Courtesy of www.weddingband.com.* Mounting only: $1,380.

Lady's 18K gold and diamond mounting with 1 **brilliant** of .02 ct total weight designed by J. A. Bevaqua. *Courtesy of www.weddingband.com.* Mounting only: $780.

22

Two-tone gold engagement ring set with a round **brilliant** diamond designed by ArtCarved. *Courtesy of www.weddingband.com.*

Today, diamonds are cut into many shapes besides round. In the mid-twentieth century, with new cutting techniques available, popular shapes for the major stones have included **oval, pear, marquise, emerald,** and **heart** shapes and for the side stones **baguette** (rectangular) and **brilliant** (round).

Classic styles of diamond engagement rings designed by Tiffany & Co. Top to bottom: **marquise, pear, emerald cut, oval,** and **round** shaped stones. *Courtesy of Diamond Information Center. Photography by Jim Bastardo.*

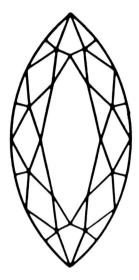

Marquise shape

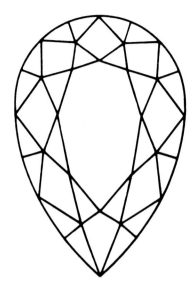

Pear or tear-drop shape

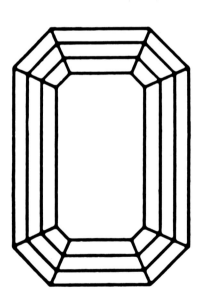

Emerald shape

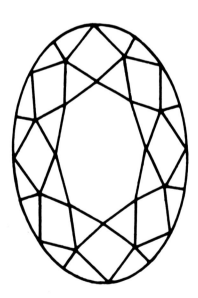

Oval shape

Lady's platinum and diamond mounting with 6 **brilliants** of .18 ct total weight and 2 **baguettes** of .18 ct total weight designed by Elber-Rosenthal Ltd. *Courtesy of www.weddingband.com.* Mounting only: $ 2,700.

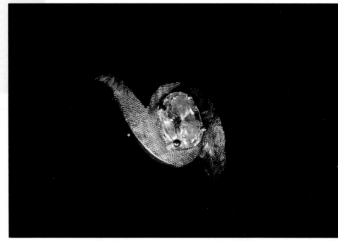

Gold and diamond ring with **oval** stone set in prongs, c.1965. *Courtesy of Blair Loughrey.*

Above: **Pear shaped diamonds**. Victorian 18K gold three-stone ring with two prong set side diamonds of pear shape, English, c.1880. *Courtesy James Robinson, NY, NY.* $10,000 - 12,000.

Left: **Pear shaped** diamond. *Courtesy Diamond Information Center.*

25

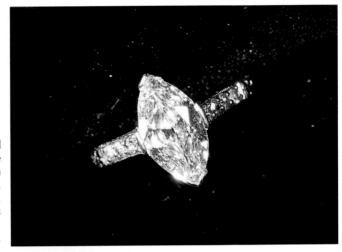

Marquise shaped diamond. Marquise diamond ring in platinum mounting, American, c.1920. *Courtesy James Robinson, NY, NY.* $16,500 - 19,800.

Left & Below: **Marquise shape stone**. American platinum, diamond, and sapphire ring with center marquise shape diamond approx. 1.27 ct bezel set, callibre sapphires cut to fit the design, engraved shank, c.1920. *Courtesy James Robinson, NY, NY.* $12,000 - 14,400.

26

Side **marquise-cut** diamonds in a ring with approximately 2 ct center round diamond. *Courtesy James Robinson, NY, NY.*

Marquise-cut diamond in a two-tone gold engagement ring designed by ArtCarved. *Courtesy of www.weddingband.com.*

Marquise-cut diamond in a two-tone gold engagement ring designed by ArtCarved. *Courtesy of www.weddingband.com.*

Lady's 18K gold mounting with yellow gold center and white gold edges designed by Bagley & Hotchkiss. *Courtesy of www.weddingband.com.* Mounting only: $920.

27

Square-cut diamond. *Courtesy Diamond Information Center.*

Platinum, diamond, and emerald three-stone ring with two **square-cut** diamonds, made by Cartier.

28

Belgian cut melee G color, VS grade diamond in a platinum and 18K gold engagement ring mounting with 10 brilliant round diamonds of 0.42 ct total weight designed by Mark Michael Designs. *Courtesy of www.weddingband.com.* $1,600.

Emerald cut diamond. American platinum and emerald cut diamond ring with side mountings, c.1925. *Courtesy James Robinson, NY, NY.* $13,750 - 16,500.

Lady's platinum and diamond mounting with 2 **baguettes** of 0.28 ct total weight designed by Elber-Rosenthal Ltd. *Courtesy of www.weddingband.com.* Mounting only: $ 2,310.

Lady's platinum and diamond mounting with 4 **baguettes** of 0.35 ct total weight designed by Elber-Rosenthal Ltd. *Courtesy of www.weddingband.com.* Mounting only: $ 2,475.

29

Platinum and diamond ring with **baguettes**, c.1970. *Courtesy of Blair Loughrey.*

14 baguette diamonds in a lady's 18K gold mounting with diamonds of 0.84 ct total weight designed by Bagley & Hotchkiss. *Courtesy of www.weddingband.com.* Mounting only: $3,865.

Lady's 18K gold and platinum diamond mounting with 4 **baguettes** of 0.73 ct total weight designed by Martin Flyer. *Courtesy of www.weddingband.com.* Mounting only: $2,400.

Lady's 18K gold and platinum mounting with 4 **baguettes** and 2 **brilliant** diamonds of 0.70 ct total weight designed by Martin Flyer. *Courtesy of www.weddingband.com.* Mounting only: $ 2,450.

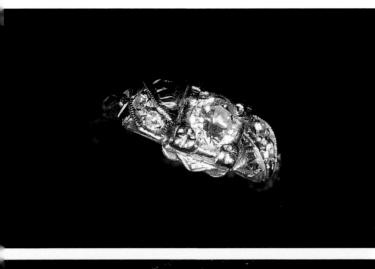

Platinum and diamond ring with four side **brilliant** diamonds, c.1930. *Courtesy of Blair Loughrey.*

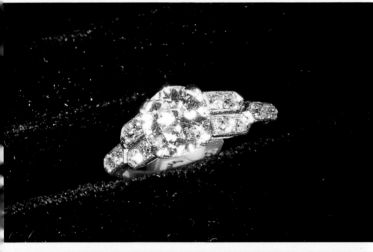

Platinum and diamond ring with approximately 1 ct center diamond and side **brilliant** diamonds. *Courtesy James Robinson, NY, NY.*

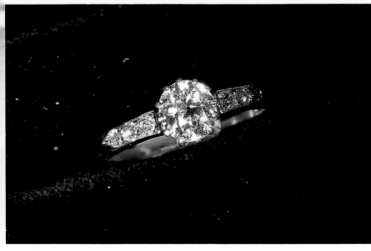

Gold and diamond ring with approximately 0.75 ct center diamond and side **brilliant** diamonds. *Courtesy James Robinson, NY, NY.*

31

Many people talk about diamond **chips** when they mean the very small stones used for decoration in jewelry. The diamond cutter hates this word: These are usually **single-cut** diamonds. Single cuts have 17 facets made up of a table, 8 facets above the girdle, and eight facets below the girdle, but have no culet facet.

New Shapes

Recently in the late twentieth century, several new shapes have emerged and many of them are patented. The new shapes for primary stones include **radiant** (rectangular), **princess** (square quadrillion), **144-facet** (round), and **dream** (marquise). Side stones also appear in new shapes: **trilliant** (triangular) and **brilliant cut baguette** (straight or tapered).

14K gold and diamond tension set mounting with 12 **Princess-cut** diamonds of 1.26 ct total weight designed by Gelin and Abaci Inc. *Courtesy of www.weddingband.com.* Mounting only: $4,275.

Princess-cut diamonds in a platinum, 18K gold, and diamond mounting with 2 princess cut diamonds of 0.15 ct total weight designed by Tacori. *Courtesy of www.weddingband.com.* Mounting only: $2,350.

Platinum, 22K yellow gold, and diamond mounting with 20 diamonds of 0.10 ct total weight designed by Tacori. *Courtesy of www.weddingband.com.* Mounting only: $1,630.

2 **trilliants** and 6 **brilliants** of 0.54 ct total weight in a platinum, 22K yellow gold, and diamond mounting designed by Tacori. *Courtesy of www.weddingband.com.* Mounting only: $2,775.

Opposite: **Modern styles** of diamond engagement rings. **Top to bottom:** (1) Channel set **emerald-cut** diamond set in matt white gold designed by Stephen Dixon of Electrum for Aaron Faber. (2) **Marquise-cut** diamond set in platinum and 18kt gold designed by Judith Conway for Aaron Faber. (3) Nina ring with **round-cut** diamond solitaire set in white gold on a single band with pave diamonds designed by H. Stern. (4) Nina ring with **round-cut** diamond set in matt yellow gold on double band with pave diamonds designed by H. Stern. (5) Solitaire **princess-cut** diamond ring in 18kt yellow gold designed by H. Stern. *Courtesy of Diamond Information Center.* Photograph by Jim Bastardo.

2 **trilliants** of 0.50 ct total weight in a platinum, 18K yellow gold, and diamond mounting designed by Tacori. *Courtesy of www.weddingband.com.* Mounting only: $2,890.

33

5 **Ideal Cut brilliants** of 0.14 ct total weight in a man's diamond wedding band designed by Mark Michael Designs. *Courtesy of www.weddingband.com.* Mounting only: $ 1,110.

Belgian-cut melee G color, VS grade diamond in a platinum and 18K gold engagement ring with 8 **brilliant** round diamonds of 0.33 ct total weight designed by Mark Michael Designs. *Courtesy of www.weddingband.com.* $1,725.

Colors

Diamonds are found in many natural colors ranging from colorless to black. The most common color used for jewelry is colorless or "white" tending toward yellow. Pastel blue, pink, yellow, red, dark blue, and black are very rare and are called "fancies." These are more expensive than "white" diamonds of similar clarity, cut, and carat weight.

A relative scale has been established to grade natural diamond colors, ranging from the colorless or "white" classification to light yellowish.

GIA*	AGS**	Description
DEF	0, 1	Colorless, exceptional white, rare white
GHIJ	2-5	Near colorless, fine white, slightly tinted white
KLM	5-7	Faint yellowish tint
NOPQR	7-9	Very light yellowish tint
STUVWXYZ	9-10	Tinted light yellowish

* A scale determined by the Gemological Institute of America (GIA)
** A scale determined by the American Gemological Society (AGS)

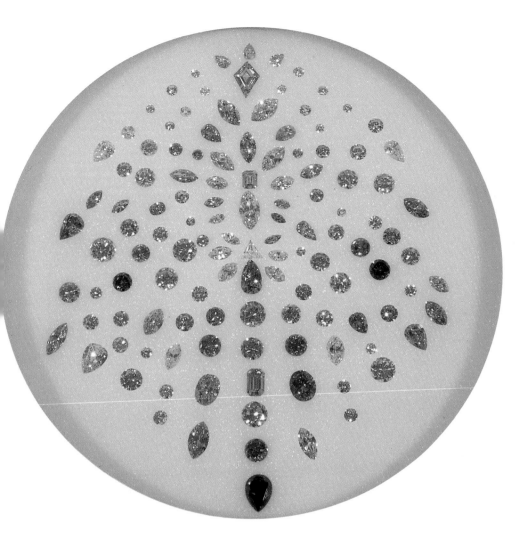

The DeBeers Collection of fancy diamonds. © DeBeers.

Therefore, an "F" rated diamond is considered more valuable than an "L" rated diamond of similar clarity, cut, and carat weight.

Another color characteristic is "**fluorescence**" which appears as lightly tinted blue and can mask a yellow tint in daylight or fluorescent light. A yellowish stone that has strong blue fluorescence is called a **premier** diamond. It looks whiter than normal and it always has an oily appearance in daylight or fluorescent light. The amount of fluorescence and oily appearance will affect the value of the diamond.

Above: **Fancy colored diamond**. American cluster yellow gold and diamond ring with large center diamond of fancy cinnamon color surrounded by ten white prong set diamonds, c.1930. *Courtesy James Robinson, NY, NY.* $12,000 - 14,400.

Right: Gold and diamond ring designed by Maison Vever, c.1890. *Courtesy of Tadema Gallery, London.*

Color enhancement

Color can be altered in diamonds. For thousands of years, even before diamonds were cut, man has known that methods can be used to bring out or improve a diamond's color. Today, a well-accepted technique for enhancing the color of diamonds is to subject them to atomic radiation. In their natural state, colored diamonds can be very rare and expensive. Irradiated diamonds are far more affordable.

Clarity and Perfection

The clarity of a diamond, or its relative lack of imperfections, is a major factor in determining a diamond's value. You may ask "How nearly flawless is the diamond?" Almost all diamonds are found with some external and internal flaws in a wide range of combinations. The Federal Trade Commission has ruled that a diamond may not be sold as flawless if it shows any inclusions to a trained eye when magnified ten times under ideal lighting conditions. What we call **flaws** or **inclusions** are naturally occurring specks found in the stone. By using a 10X loupe, available at all jewelry shops and optical stores, you can learn what to look for.

There are many kinds, sizes, and colors of flaws and inclusions and they all have varying effects on the value of the diamond. It is a complicated business. The value will be affected depending on the size and position of the flaw.

Assorted diamonds. *Courtesy Diamond Information Center.*

External flaws and blemishes include:

A Natural- a rough, unpolished area of the crystal that may look fuzzy white. If a "natural" is polished, it may appear as an extra facet (see Cuts).

A Nick- a small chip in the stone.

Girdle roughness- cross-hatched lines at the girdle, which can be removed by polishing.

Pits and cavities- indentations on the table facet.

A scratch- a minor line across a surface, which can be removed by polishing.

Internal flaws, called **inclusions**, include:

A dark spot- caused by crystal or metallic substance.

Pinpoint- dot or cluster of dots that look whitish.

Cleavage- a crack with a flat plane, that can split open.

Colorless crystal- diamond or mineral.

Feather- a crack with irregular shape.

Girdle fringes- small cracks at the girdle, which can be removed by polishing.

Graining- growth lines, two to four pale brown lines.

Knaat or twin lines- ridges of uneven shape.

This relative scale grades natural diamond clarity from flawless down to imperfect.

GIA*	AGS**	Description
F or FL0		flawless
IF	1	internally flawless
VVS-1		
VVS-2	2	very, very small inclusions
VS-1	3	
VS-2	4	very small inclusions
SI-1	5	small inclusions
SI-2	6	
I-1	7	imperfect
I-2	8,9	
I-3	10	

* A scale determined by the Gemological Institute of America (GIA)
** A scale determined by the American Gemological Society (AGS)

Therefore, a VVS-1 clarity grade diamond is worth more than a VS-2 diamond of the same color, cut and carat weight.

If the internal flaws are positioned so that they cannot be seen from the table, they will have a less adverse effect on the grade and value of the stone. A good stone cutter may be able to position the flaws in a more advantageous place. Prongs can be positioned by a careful stone setter to obscure the flaws.

Clarity enhancement

Clarity sometimes can be enhanced in diamonds by techniques called "laser drilling" and "fracture filling." These enhancements make a diamond less valuable than a comparable, unaltered diamond.

As a safeguard to the consumer, the World Federation of Diamond Manufacturers Association and the World Federation of Diamond Bourses have passed a resolution mandating that diamond merchants disclose the existence of laser drilling in stones they sell. The resolution, adopted in July of 1998, reads as follows:

> Although laser drilling is an acceptable, permanent process utilized in the cutting and polishing of diamonds, and does not infuse a foreign substance into a diamond or otherwise affect its integrity, it is nevertheless required that this process be disclosed in writing when diamonds are offered for sale. This resolution shall go into effect as of January 1, 1999. (Matthew Wilde, "World Diamond Congress Tackles Lasering," *Rapaport Diamond Report*, Vol. 21, No. 30, August 7, 1998, p.1)

In "laser drilling," the intense heat of a laser beam is used to open a minute channel in the diamond to the point of a natural internal black spot, which either vaporizes the spot or allows a channel where solutions can be introduced that will permanently whiten the spot to make it less noticeable. The path of the laser beam is left in the diamond.

In "fracture filling," a transparent substance is introduced into a fracture in the diamond, but the filling is not permanent and may need to be replaced when it discolors.

Carat Weight

To measure the weight of gold and gems, a standard was developed in ancient times in the seeds of the carob fruit; one seed weighed one "carat." Today, the standard measurement for diamond weight is the **carat** (abbreviated "ct"), not to be confused with the word **karat** (starts with a "k," abbreviated "k") which is the standard measurement for pure gold.

Today, one carat is equivalent to 200 milligrams (mg) or 1/5 of a gram. Therefore, 5 carats = 1 gram = 1,000 mg. There are 100 "**points**" per carat weight, so 100 "points" = 1 carat.

It is easy to confuse the *weight* of a diamond with the *size* of a diamond because they are closely related measurements. Different cuts of diamonds are deeper or wider, and therefore

Diamonds of graduated weights, approximate weights, left to right, *Courtesy James Robinson, NY, NY.*:
2 ct diamond, American platinum ring c.1935. $24,500 - 29,400.
1 ct diamond, American platinum ring c.1930. $9,875 - 11,850.
0.75 ct diamond, American 14K gold ring c.1890. $4,500 - 5,400.
0.40 ct diamond, bezel set c.1900. $2,200 - 2,640.

may appear to be larger or smaller, regardless of the actual weight of the stone. When someone refers to a 2-carat diamond, they are talking about its weight, not its size.

Many more smaller diamonds are found than larger ones. In South Africa, for example, over twenty tons of sand and gravel are mined to get two carats of diamond fit for use in jewelry, and by the time this diamond is cut and polished, there will be only one carat of finished gems. This is the average for all sizes, large and small. However, the larger stones are so much more rare than the smaller diamonds that 250 tons of sand and gravel must be mined to get a rough diamond big enough to produce a finished one-carat gem. For this reason, larger diamonds of the same quality are much more valuable per carat. A one-carat stone is worth a great deal more than two half-carat stones of equal quality.

The term "**spread**" is used in the jewelry field to refer to the size a stone **appears** to be when its diameter is compared with the chart for perfectly proportioned cut diamonds. However, a "spread" of one carat does not mean a "weight" of one carat, but (since most stones are not perfectly proportioned) usually less. Do not let the term fool or confuse you.

Diamond Grading Reports

Diamonds of one carat weight and above can be graded by a professionally recognized testing laboratory, which is highly recommended. The results of the diamond grading report can serve many purposes, and the numbered and dated certificate that accompanies the testing results can be transferred to the diamond's subsequent owners as a record of the diamond's history. As a whole, the information determines the identity of the diamond and can be used to differentiate it from almost any other. This identity can also help in the finding of matching stones, if desired.

For reference, here is a sample certificate. The following information should be included:

- **Identity** of the stone: Diamond.
- **Weight**: exact weight in carats.
- **Dimensions**: very precise measurements of two diameters, a high and a low, in millimeters to the hundredth place. These measurements will identify out-of-round stones.
- **Proportion**: including the depth and table percentages.
- **Finish**: comments about the polish and symmetry.
- **Girdle thickness**: if the girdle is too thick or too thin.
- **Culet**: size, it should be small.
- **Color**: the color grade from colorless to tinted.
- **Clarity**: internal and external, ranging from flawless to imperfect.
- **Table percentage**: the width of the table as a percent of the width of the stone; 53-58% is considered the best range.
- **Depth percentage**: The distance from the table to the culet as a percentage of the width of the stone; 58-60% is considered the best range.
- **Crown angle**: the angle at which the crown has been cut; 30-36 degrees is considered the best range, with 36 the optimal.
- **Fluorescence**: mentioned if present, including the color (blue, yellow, or white) and rated weak, moderate, strong, or very strong.

Reputable gem testing laboratories are located in many parts of the world and are easily accessible to the public and the jewelry industry. Among the most widely known are the Gemological Institute of America in New York and Carlbad, California, and the American Gemological Society in New York. (See also Chapter 4, Written Guarantees.)

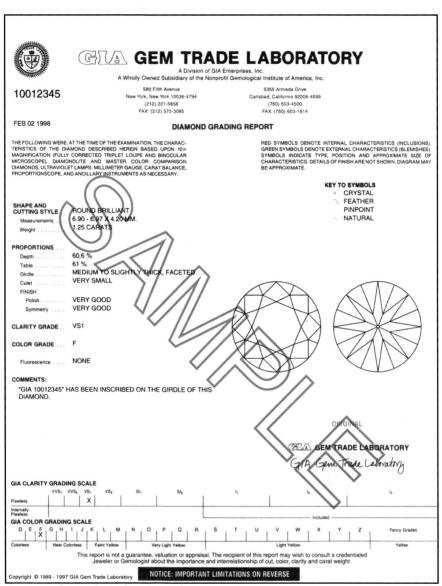

GIA GEM TRADE LABORATORY

A Division of GIA Enterprises, Inc.
A Wholly Owned Subsidiary of the Nonprofit Gemological Institute of America, Inc.

10012345

580 Fifth Avenue
New York, New York 10036-4794
(212) 221-5858
FAX: (212) 575-3095

5355 Armada Drive
Carlsbad, California 92008-4699
(760) 603-4500
FAX: (760) 603-1814

FEB 02 1998

DIAMOND GRADING REPORT

THE FOLLOWING WERE, AT THE TIME OF THE EXAMINATION, THE CHARAC-TERISTICS OF THE DIAMOND DESCRIBED HEREIN BASED UPON 10x MAGNIFICATION (FULLY CORRECTED TRIPLET LOUPE AND BINOCULAR MICROSCOPE), DIAMONDLITE AND MASTER COLOR COMPARISON DIAMONDS, ULTRAVIOLET LAMPS, MILLIMETER GAUGE, CARAT BALANCE, PROPORTIONSCOPE, AND ANCILLARY INSTRUMENTS AS NECESSARY.

RED SYMBOLS DENOTE INTERNAL CHARACTERISTICS (INCLUSIONS). GREEN SYMBOLS DENOTE EXTERNAL CHARACTERISTICS (BLEMISHES). SYMBOLS INDICATE TYPE, POSITION AND APPROXIMATE SIZE OF CHARACTERISTICS. DETAILS OF FINISH ARE NOT SHOWN. DIAGRAM MAY BE APPROXIMATE.

KEY TO SYMBOLS
- ○ CRYSTAL
- ⌐ FEATHER
- PINPOINT
- ⌢ NATURAL

SHAPE AND CUTTING STYLE . . . ROUND BRILLIANT
Measurements . . . 6.90 - 6.97 X 4.20 MM.
Weight . . . . 1.25 CARATS

PROPORTIONS . . .
Depth . . . . 60.6 %
Table . . . . 61 %
Girdle . . . . MEDIUM TO SLIGHTLY THICK, FACETED
Culet . . . . VERY SMALL
FINISH
Polish . . . . VERY GOOD
Symmetry . . . . . VERY GOOD

CLARITY GRADE . . VS1

COLOR GRADE . . . F

Fluorescence . . . . NONE

COMMENTS:
"GIA 10012345" HAS BEEN INSCRIBED ON THE GIRDLE OF THIS DIAMOND.

ORIGINAL

GIA GEM TRADE LABORATORY

GIA Gem Trade Laboratory

GIA CLARITY GRADING SCALE

Flawless	VVS₁	VVS₂	VS₁	VS₂	SI₁	SI₂	I₁	I₂	I₃
			X						

Internally Flawless — Included

GIA COLOR GRADING SCALE

D	E	F	G	H	I	J	K	L	M	N	O	P	Q	R	S	T	U	V	W	X	Y	Z	Fancy Grades
	X																						
Colorless			Near Colorless				Faint Yellow			Very Light Yellow					Light Yellow							Yellow

This report is not a guarantee, valuation or appraisal. The recipient of this report may wish to consult a credentialed Jeweler or Gemologist about the importance and interrelationship of cut, color, clarity and carat weight.

Copyright © 1989 - 1997 GIA Gem Trade Laboratory

NOTICE: IMPORTANT LIMITATIONS ON REVERSE

Courtesy of Gemological Institute of America.

Diamond grading reports should be inspected carefully to detect any irregularities or alterations that might indicate a counterfeit certificate or fictitious testing agency. You should be able to verify the authenticity of the certificate by calling the issuing grading laboratory and referring to the certificate number and date of inspection. A reputable laboratory or appraiser can verify the information for you and a reputable jeweler will have the stone recertified by a recognized testing laboratory. By following these steps you can be confident that you are getting an accurate description of the diamond. They will also help you to better determine the fair value of the diamond.

Diamond grading reports can also serve to identify particular stones for matching purposes and for the identification of stolen merchandise. (Also see Chapter 4, Written Guarantees.)

In 1998, new technology brought innovation to the diamond industry with the development of a machine to identify specific diamonds over 0.05 carats, both loose and mounted. **Gemprint** is a computerized identification system for diamonds in which a high beam of light is sent through a diamond so that the stone's unique brightest sparkles can be mapped against a square screen. A computer scans the sparkles as a specific pattern, like a "fingerprint" of the stone, and makes a paper print of the scan. Law enforcement agencies expect to be able to use the system to help identify stolen diamonds more precisely.

Another innovation of the late 1990s is the use of marking diamonds with tiny trademark and identifying insignia. This type of innovation may make product identity an important factor in future diamond markets.

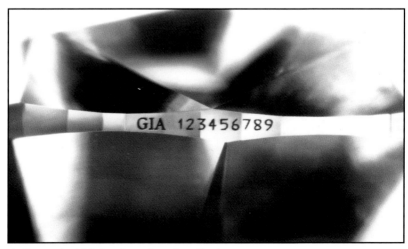

44

A diamond which has been laser inscribed.
Courtesy Gemological Institute of America.

Diamond Imitations

The lure of true diamonds over the centuries has challenged man to find a substitute: a substance easier to obtain which can be made at will for a lower cost. Glass has provided some possibilities and extensive efforts have been made to improve the quality of glass and its shaping and cutting to approximate the various qualities of diamonds. The development of glass substitutes for diamond has become an important part of glass history. Imitation diamonds have been successfully manufactured for industrial use by the General Electric Company and other companies through laboratory control of the physical and chemical characteristics that make diamonds in nature. The resulting **synthetic diamonds** provide important alternatives to natural diamonds in world industries.

Among the commercial imitations for gem-quality diamonds are **glass rhinestones**, which have become an industry of their own to supply the imitation diamond and other gemstone market. Imitation diamonds known as **Wellington Diamonds** and **Fabulite** are trade names for strontium titanate which displays even more flash than true diamonds. A close imitation diamond on the market is **cubic zirconia**, often called CZ for short. Anther imitation is **GGG**, gadolinium gallium garnet, which has many characteristics similar to diamonds. **YAG**, yttrium aluminum garnet, is hard but lacks the fire of diamonds. **Synthetic sapphire** and **synthetic spinel** are nearly as hard as diamonds but have a less reflecting flash.

These imitations can provide desirable alternatives to diamonds when their identity is revealed and acknowledged by all parties in a transaction.

2 *Colored Stones and Pearls*

Engagement rings with colored stones and pearls are quite beautiful, whether the colored stones are mounted by themselves or in combination with diamonds. Some prefer the colors and different appearances other gems provide. There are many colored stones to choose from, and jewelers can show you a rainbow of shades, many shapes, and a progression of sizes.

Cabochon colored gems in gold rings designed by Rebecca Myers. *Courtesy of www.weddingband.com.*

Gemstone Identification Report

Gemstones can be tested by qualified laboratories that issue identification reports. For example, the Gemological Insititute of America provides analysis of colored gems with detailed descriptions of the results. A jeweler can request this service for the customer.

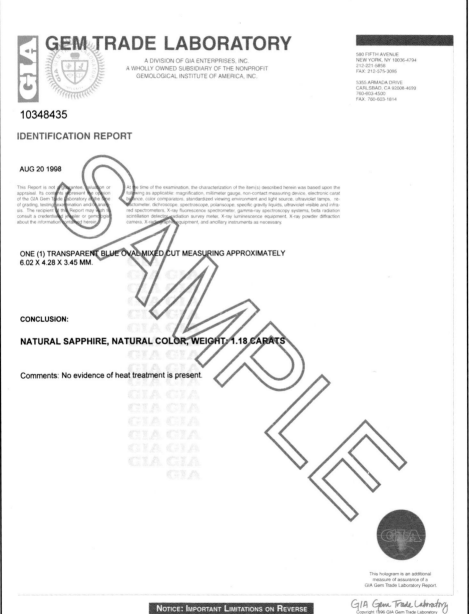

GEM TRADE LABORATORY

A DIVISION OF GIA ENTERPRISES, INC.
A WHOLLY OWNED SUBSIDIARY OF THE NONPROFIT
GEMOLOGICAL INSTITUTE OF AMERICA, INC.

580 FIFTH AVENUE
NEW YORK, NY 10036-4794
212-221-5858
FAX: 212-575-3095

5355 ARMADA DRIVE
CARLSBAD, CA 92008-4699
760-603-4500
FAX: 760-603-1814

10348435

IDENTIFICATION REPORT

AUG 20 1998

This Report is not a guarantee, valuation or appraisal. Its contents represent the opinion of the GIA Gem Trade Laboratory at the time of grading, testing, examination and/or analysis. The recipient of this Report may wish to consult a credentialed jeweler or gemologist about the information contained herein.

At the time of the examination, the characterization of the item(s) described herein was based upon the following as applicable: magnification, millimeter gauge, non-contact measuring device, electronic carat balance, color comparators, standardized viewing environment and light source, ultraviolet lamps, refractometer, dichroscope, spectroscope, polariscope, specific gravity liquids, ultraviolet-visible and infrared spectrometers, X-ray fluorescence spectrometer, gamma-ray spectroscopy systems, beta radiation scintillation detector, radiation survey meter, X-ray luminescence equipment, X-ray powder diffraction camera, X-radiographic equipment, and ancillary instruments as necessary.

ONE (1) TRANSPARENT BLUE OVAL MIXED CUT MEASURING APPROXIMATELY
6.02 X 4.28 X 3.45 MM.

CONCLUSION:

NATURAL SAPPHIRE, NATURAL COLOR, WEIGHT: 1.18 CARATS

Comments: No evidence of heat treatment is present.

This hologram is an additional measure of assurance of a GIA Gem Trade Laboratory Report.

NOTICE: IMPORTANT LIMITATIONS ON REVERSE

GIA Gem Trade Laboratory
Copyright 1996 GIA Gem Trade Laboratory

Courtesy Gemological Institute of America.

Color Groups

If your preference is toward a particular color, the following list of colored stones in their color groups may be useful to you during your search for an engagement ring.

GREEN
Alexandrite
Demantoid Garnet
Emerald
Peridot
Green Sapphire
Tourmaline
Tsavorite Garnet
Zircon

YELLOW
Beryl
Chrysoberyl
Citrine
Yellow Sapphire
Zircon

ORANGE
Mexican Opal
Orange Sapphire
Spinel
Topaz
Tourmaline
Zircon

RED
Garnet
Morganite
Pink Sapphire
Rubellite
Ruby
Spinel
Tourmaline
Zircon

Modern 18K gold, **tourmaline**, and diamond ring. *Courtesy James Robinson, NY, NY.* $3,400 - 4,080.

Winged globe ring of gold and cabochon **garnet** designed by William Thomas Pavitt, English, c.1905. *Courtesy of Tadema Gallery, London.*

Left: Two rings with diamond accents and prong-set emerald-cut colored stones. The **red** stone is **tourmaline** and the **brown** stone is **citrine**. *Private collection.*

Below: Platinum, **blue sapphire**, and diamond three-stone ring, c.1930. *Courtesy James Robinson, NY, NY.* $8,500 - 10,200.

VIOLET
Amethyst
Morganite
Rhodolite
Sapphire
Spinel

BLUE
Aquamarine
Blue Sapphire
Morganite
Spinel
Tanzanite
Topaz
Zircon

WHITE
Pearl
Mother of Pearl
Shell

Among the colored gems in the list above, a few are very popular for engagement rings and you may want a little more information about them individually.

49

Above: Platinum, diamond, and **emerald** three-stone ring with two square-cut diamonds, made by Cartier.

Left: **Emerald**, platinum, and diamond lady's mounting with 28 brilliant cut diamonds of 0.41 ct total weight and 4 round emeralds of 0.10 ct total weight designed by Elber-Rosenthal Ltd. *Courtesy of www.weddingband.com.* Mounting only: $ 2,590.

Emerald is a beryllium-aluminum silicate with traces of chromium or vanadium oxides which give an emerald its rich assortment of green colors. Emerald is somewhat softer than rubies and sapphires making it somewhat risky to mount as a ring without some risk to its edges. Therefore, it is sometimes flanked or surrounded by diamonds.

Emerald is one of the most valuable gemstones. Since ancient times, emeralds have been mined in southeastern Egypt. Today, the finest emeralds are found in Columbia, Brazil, the Ural mountains of Russia, and in central Africa.

Emerald Traditions

Emerald is the birthstone for May, symbolizing hope and the coming of Spring. It is the special stone for Wednesday and the zodiac sign Cancer (June 21 to July 22). Emerald has been called the symbol of life, agriculture, and abundant nature.

In the first century, the Roman scholar Pliny wrote: "no stone is more delightful to the eye, for whereas the sight fixes itself with avidity upon the green grass and the foliage of the trees, we have all the more pleasure of looking upon the emerald."

Romans believed that by gazing upon the emerald, one could restore weary or dimmed eyesight.

In medieval times, emeralds were used as a cure for eye disease and to guard against the evil eye and epilepsy.

In the Orient, emeralds represented immortality and courage.

The transparent red variety of corundum is called ruby after the Latin adjective meaning "red." It is composed of about 75 percent oxide of aluminum (alumina crystal), 17 percent magnesia and 4 percent iron, in addition to trace quantities of silica and minor elements. These minor elements and the amount of iron determine the various shades of red from light rose to deep carmine. The best quality color is a deep shade of clear red called "pigeon's blood." The light pink varieties are called pink sapphires. Blue varieties of corundum are called sapphires.

Rubies of small size have been found in many parts of the world, but one famous location is Burma where rubies of large size and magnificent color have originated.

Because a fine, gem-quality ruby is rarer than a diamond of the same size, rubies are among the most valuable of all gems.

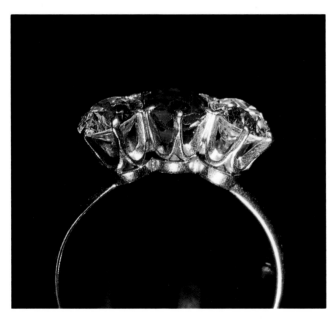

Gold, diamond, and **ruby** three-stone ring with two round diamonds.

Ruby Traditions

Ruby is the birthstone for both July and December and the special gem of Sunday and the zodiac sign Capricorn (December 21 to January 21). To the Greeks, ruby was thought of as living coal, as though red hot coals were made into stone. In a Hebrew legend, ruby symbolized the boy Reuben whose conduct to his father made him blush.

The name sapphire is most frequently associated with a transparent, deep blue shade of corundum, but many other colors of sapphire exist including white, which resembles diamond, and a shade of red called ruby.

Four colors of blue sapphire. Left to right: Medium blue, dark blue, light blue, Kashmir blue considered preferable by the English. *Courtesy James Robinson, NY, NY.*

Blue sapphires are composed of 98.5 percent alumina, 1 percent oxide of iron, 0.5 percent lime, and trace oxides. The oxide of cobalt determines the popular deep blue color. Sapphires are quite hard and dense, and their color can be darkened by intense heat.

Sapphires have been found since ancient times in Ceylon and the stones are traditionally from Burma and India. In Thailand, the Hill of Precious Stones has become famous for their fine sapphires. Recently, light blue sapphires have come from the Helena area of Montana, in the United States, and other fine specimens from Queensland, Australia.

Traditionally, the preferred shade of blue sapphire, especially in Europe, is a clear medium blue called Kashmir. In recent times, sapphires have been particularly popular choices for engagement rings ever since Diana, the Princess of Wales, accepted a sapphire surrounded by diamonds from Prince Charles.

18K gold, Kashmir sapphire, and diamond ring, c.1900. *Courtesy James Robinson, NY, NY.*

Ring in gold set with a cabochon **sapphire**, designed
by Archibald Knox for Liberty & Co., London, c.1900.
Courtesy of Tadema Gallery, London.

Sapphire Traditions

Sapphire is the birthstone for April (along with diamond) and the special stone for Saturday and the zodiac sign Taurus (April 20 to May 21).

Greek scholars believed that seafarers were protected on long journeys across the waters by sapphires. Ever since then, good luck at sea is credited to the sapphire.

Platinum, cabochon **sapphire**, and diamond ring, English, c.1925. *Courtesy James Robinson, NY, NY.* $29,500 - 35,400.

Superstition also looks to the sapphire to determine the fidelity of a spouse: Many sources claim the sapphire refuses to shine for the unchaste. Rather, it will change color in the presence of the cheated partner. As a result of this reasoning a tradition of priests wearing sapphires emerged. In the twelfth century, Pope Innocent III declared that gold and unengraved sapphires should be used to symbolize pontifical rank.

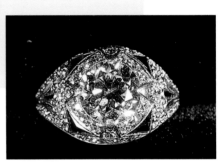

Above & right: American Art Deco platinum, diamond, and **sapphire** ring, center brilliant diamond collet set with four triangular sapphires, made c.1930 by S. Kind & Son, Philadelphia. *Courtesy James Robinson, NY, NY.*

Platinum, diamond, and **sapphire** mounting with 22 brilliants of 0.34 ct total weight and 12 squarish sapphires of 0.46 ct total weight designed by Infinity Line. *Courtesy of www.weddingband.com.* Mounting only: $1,875

Lady's platinum and sapphire mounting with 4 French-cut **sapphires** of 1/3 ct total weight designed by Elber-Rosenthal Ltd. *Courtesy of www.weddingband.com.* Mounting only: $ 1,615.

55

Pearl

Gem-quality pearls are naturally produced in several colors by a saltwater, non-edible oyster and a variety of freshwater oysters. Since ancient times, they have been found in many places of the world, from the Persian Gulf to the waters of the South Seas, the north coast of Australia, and the Pacific waters of Venezuela, Panama, Mexico, and Southern California.

56

Mistletoe ring of gold with **pearls** designed by Saint-Yves, France, c.1900. *Courtesy of Tadema Gallery, London.*

A pearl is composed entirely of calcium carbonate particles arranged in overlapping layers and bound together with organic material produced by the oysters. When an irritating foreign particle, which could be a piece of sand, a parasite, worm, or small fish, enters the oyster, the creature responds by covering the irritant with smooth layers of body material and an iridescent layer, called nacre; over time these build up to form a pearl. Rarely are pearls uniformly round, but those that are, if of large size, are very expensive.

Pearls are measured in weight by a unit called a **grain**; there are four grains in a carat and twenty grains in a gram. Their sizes are measured in **millimeters**.

The origin of a pearl distinguishes its type. **Natural pearls** are completely oyster-made, not helped by man. **Oriental pearls** are natural, saltwater pearls from the Persian Gulf, which was the primary source for natural pearls up to the last hundred years. **Freshwater pearls** come from oysters living in rivers. **Baroque pearls** are formed when the nacre builds up in irregular layers, causing interesting and often iridescent, non-uniform pearls. **French pearls** is a term used recently to identify irregular pieces of oyster shell with some of the characteristics of natural pearls. **Seed pearls** are tiny round pearls, usually under 2 mm in size; these were popular in the last century but are rare today.

Cultured pearls are made by oysters with the help of mankind, such as man's introduction of a carefully placed and precisely designed foreign particle to sea-living oysters. Cultured pearls have become an important commercial industry throughout the world, particularly in Japan over the last fifty years. **Blister pearls** form either naturally or with man's help, and are permanently attached to the shell of the oyster so that part of the shell remains intact. **Mabé pearls** are dome shaped due to man's involvement in their formation, placing a plastic form into an oyster shell so that the

Pearl and platinum ring with side diamond baguettes.

nacre can form over it. These can be made in large quantity at a relative low cost, but are more fragile than natural pearls. Each of these pearl types can be used to their own advantage in various jewelry designs.

The colors of pearls vary from snow white to dark, known as black, with many attractive shades of pink, blue, green and grey. The characteristic iridescence of pearls can look metallic or matt. Often pearls with variations of color within the same gem are not desirable and are often cut and/or mounted to hide the variation.

Because pearls are organic, they respond to dry and hot conditions by discoloring, drying out, and cracking. By wearing them, pearls react with normal body oils to retain their reflective properties.

Pearl Traditions

Pearls are the ancient birthstone of June and are the special gems of Monday, Winter, the zodiac sign Cancer, and the celestial sign of the ocean. Their round and glowing form has caused them also to be associated with the moon.

Oriental literature relates that ancient people believed pearls to be formed when oysters rose to the surface of the water from drops of dew or from water that changed to pearls by air and sunlight. When worn at the neck, pearls are an emblem of chastity, and convey purity, innocence, and peace.

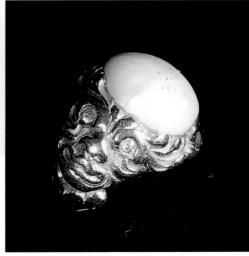

Above & right: American 14K gold, **blister pearl**, and diamond ring, c.1910. *Courtesy James Robinson, NY, NY.* $4,250 - 5,100.

3 *Your Setting*

There are many ways to mount gem stones to a ring band, and these methods are known as the **settings**. Most rings have metal settings of gold, platinum, or silver, but other metals such as brass can be used alone or in combination to make unusual settings. The variety of materials used can affect the durability and monetary value of an engagement ring.

Metals

Victorian 18K **gold** three-stone ring with two prong-set side diamonds of pear shape, English, c.1880. *Courtesy James Robinson, NY, NY.* $10,000 - 12,000.

Gold

Gold has been a coveted metal since early times. To measure the weight of gold and gems, a standard was developed in ancient times using the seeds of the carob fruit; one seed weighed one "carat." Today, in the United States, the term **karat** (spelled with a "k") refers to the weight of gold, while the term **carat** (spelled with a "c") refers to the weight of gems. The abbreviation for *karat* is "k," and for *carat* is "ct."

A pure gold coin called a "solidus" in Byzantium weighed 24 karats. Therefore, 24k became the standard mark for 100 percent pure gold. Gold is a soft metal that alone does not stand up to much wear. In jewelry, gold is usually strengthened with the addition of other metals to form an alloy. The amount of gold defines the purity of the alloy which is identified in the United States by the karat number and in Europe by the fineness number based on a scale of parts of gold per thousand, as seen in the following scale:

US Marking	Composition	European Marking
24K gold	100% gold, 0% other	999
22K gold	91.5% gold, 8.5% other	915
18K gold	75% gold, 25% other	750
14K gold	58.5% gold, 41.5% other	585
12K gold	50% gold, 50% other	500
10K gold	41.6% gold, 57.4% other	416
9K gold	38% gold, 62% other	380

18K **two-tone gold** engagement ring with diamonds of 0.50 ct total weight designed by Diana. *Courtesy of www.weddingband.com.* Mounting only: $1,400.

18K **two-tone gold** engagement ring designed by Jean-François Albert. *Courtesy of www.weddingband.com.* Mounting only: $790.

Different alloys can give the **gold color variations** from nearly pink, to yellow, to nearly white. You may find you have a preference for a particular color of gold, or find that the stones you like look better with a particular color of gold.

18K **two-tone gold** engagement ring designed by Jean-François Albert. *Courtesy of www.weddingband.com.* Mounting only: $820.

14K **gold** and diamond mounting with 4 brilliant diamonds of 0.04 ct total weight designed by Folkways. *Courtesy of www.weddingband.com.* Mounting only: $2,945.

Platinum and 18K **gold** engagement ring designed by Création Thibaudeau, Inc. *Courtesy of www.weddingband.com.* Mounting only: $975.

Gold engagement ring with diamonds designed by Baguette World. *Courtesy of www.weddingband.com.*

Gold engagement ring with diamonds designed by Baguette World. *Courtesy of www.weddingband.com.*

Lady's 18K **white gold** mounting with **yellow gold** top designed by Bagley & Hotchkiss. *Courtesy of www.weddingband.com.* Mounting only: $750.

Gold engagement ring with diamonds designed by Baguette World. *Courtesy of www.weddingband.com.*

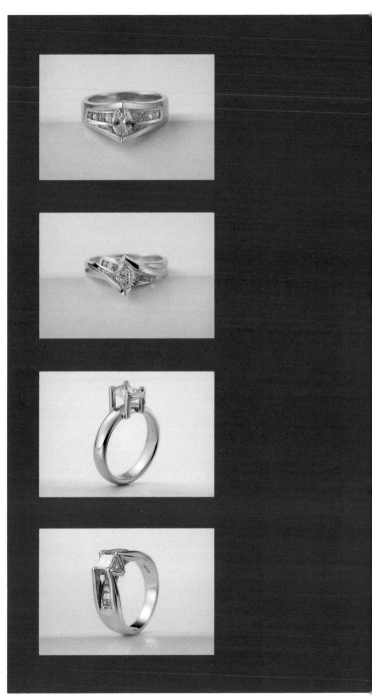

Platinum

Platinum is a strong and heavy metal, quite rare in nature and therefore more expensive than a comparable quantity of gold, for example. For added strength, platinum is often mixed with slight amounts of other metals of a similar composition. Platinum is identified on jewelry in the United States by the markings **PT** or **plat**, and in Europe by numerical markings **950** or **PT950**.

Since the beginning of the twentieth century, platinum has been used for fine jewelry. The characteristics of platinum enable it to be pulled to thin wires without loosing its strength, and this makes it a good choice for openwork designs. Platinum prongs hold gems for many years without abrasion, but platinum's higher cost than gold can be a significant factor in your choice to use it.

Lady's **platinum** mounting designed by Fusaro. *Courtesy of www.weddingband.com.* Mounting only: $855.

Lady's **platinum** mounting designed by Fusaro. *Courtesy of www.weddingband.com.* Mounting only: $1,105.

Platinum engagement ring mounting designed by Tacori. *Courtesy of www.weddingband.com.* Mounting only: $1,575.

63

Lady's **platinum** and diamond mounting with 4 brilliants of 0.08 ct total weight designed by Elber-Rosenthal Ltd. *Courtesy of www.weddingband.com.* Mounting only: $ 1,915.

Platinum engagement ring with diamonds designed by Baguette World. *Courtesy of www.weddingband.com.*

Platinum and 24K gold mounting designed by Création Thibaudeau, Inc. *Courtesy of www.weddingband.com.* Mounting only: $1,390.

Lady's **platinum** and diamond mounting with 46 brilliants of 0.38 ct total weight designed by Fusaro. *Courtesy of www.weddingband.com.* Mounting only: $3,375.

64

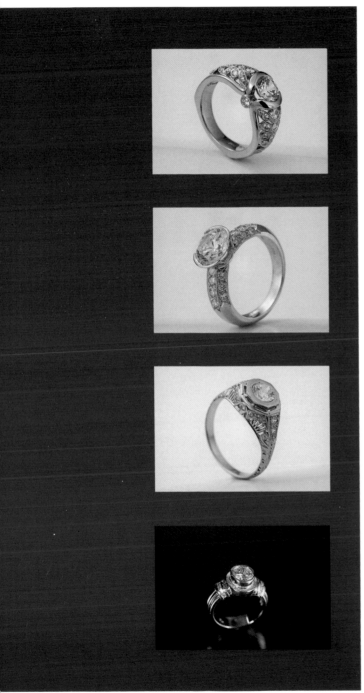

Platinum and 22K gold mounting set with 30 brilliant diamonds of 0.45 ct total weight designed by Judith Evans. *Courtesy of www.weddingband.com.* Mounting only: $2,725.

Lady's **platinum** and diamond mounting with 18 brilliants of 0.45 ct total weight designed by Fusaro. *Courtesy of www.weddingband.com.* Mounting only: $2,205.

Platinum and diamond mounting with 18 brilliants of 0.18 ct total weight designed by Infinity Line. *Courtesy of www.weddingband.com.* Mounting only: $1,050.

18K **yellow gold** ring with **platinum head** of the diamond designed by Rebecca Myers. *Courtesy of www.weddingband.com.* $21,000.

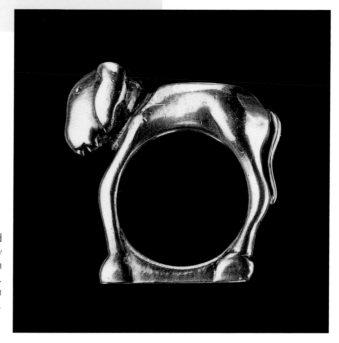

Silver ring shaped as a lamb, made by Sah and Mosheh Oved, c.1940. *Courtesy of Tadema Gallery, London.*

Silver has been used for jewelry since the eighteenth century, but only became popular after the mid-19th century. Because silver is a soft metal, it is usually mixed with slight amounts of other metals to gain strength. The amount of silver parts per thousand determines the fineness of a silver alloy. 925 parts silver per thousand is the standard alloy used for jewelry today; it is known as "sterling silver" and is marked **Sterling**. Some European silver, particularly from Germany in former times, used a different alloy with 800 parts silver; jewelry with that content is marked **800**.

14K or 18K yellow, red and white gold, sterling silver and copper **Mokume** (wood grain metal) mounting designed by George Sawyer. *Courtesy of www.weddingband.com.* Mounting only: $880 to $1890 depending on width, ring size, and metal combinations.

66

Besides the three primary metals used for settings in engagement rings already mentioned, other metals can also be used alone or in combination. Bronze, copper, brass, and nickel can be artistically used and they give a very different appearance than the stronger and more formal metals. **Mokume** is a traditional Japanese technique for combining metals that appears like wood grain. It can be quite beautiful.

Setting Styles

Over the years, different styles of engagement ring settings have emerged and become popular. Some settings have enjoyed short-lived use with specific artistic styles, while others have remained and become classic "standards," signifying the nearing wedding engagement. The following are some of the many setting styles you may find on the market.

Solitaire Settings

Open mounted ring of platinum and pearl with side diamond baguettes. *Private collection.*

Bezel (or collet) Setting

Bezel settings have a metal rim completely surrounding the single gem stone. The edges of the metal rim can be smooth, millegrained, serrated, beveled, or shaped in an original way. The back of a ring with a bezel setting can be open to let light in or be closed. Bezel settings are also called **collet** settings, especially in England.

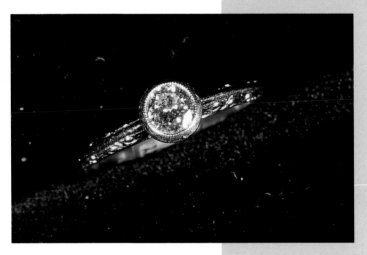

Opposite: **Bezel** setting in a ring of gold with enamel and diamond, designed by Murrle Bennett & Co., England and Germany, c.1900. *Courtesy of Tadema Gallery, London.*

Above: Platinum ring with **bezel** millegraine setting, solitaire diamond. *Courtesy James Robinson, NY, NY.*

Right: Lady's platinum **bezel** mounting holds a 6 mm round diamond only, designed by Elber-Rosenthal Ltd. *Courtesy of www.weddingband.com.* Mounting only: $1,315.

Prong Setting

Separate posts that rise to hold a gem stone are known as "prongs." Prongs can be used in many different combinations of numbers and styles to secure the stone to the ring band. Separate solitaire settings can be used together for multi-stone rings; however, in each instance the individual settings are the same as in solitaire rings. The prongs can end in different designs such as flat, pointed, round, or V-shaped.

4-prong solitaire setting with a round diamond.
Courtesy Diamond Information Center.

6-prong setting on a round, brilliant-cut solitaire diamond set in a platinum band designed by Hammerman. Courtesy of Diamond Information Center. Photograph by Jim Bastardo.

Flat prongs hold a marquise diamond in a platinum mounting, American, c.1920. *Courtesy James Robinson, NY, NY.* $16,500 - 19,800.

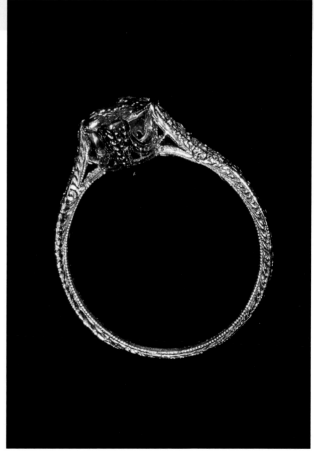

Built-up openwork setting with millegraining and **engraving on the shank** is typical of the style popular in the 1920s. American platinum and diamond ring, center diamond approx. 2.6 ct and small diamonds, c.1920. *Courtesy James Robinson, NY, NY.* $48,500 - 58,200.

73

Tension

The stone is held in place by the inward tension of the two sides of the band.

14 K gold **tension-set** mounting designed by Gelin and Abaci Inc. *Courtesy of www.weddingband. com.* Mounting only: $920.

14K gold and diamond **tension-set** mounting with 10 baguettes of 0.80 ct total weight designed by Gelin and Abaci Inc. *Courtesy of www.weddingband.com.* Mounting only: $2,625.

14 K gold and diamond **tension-set** mounting with 4 diamonds of 0.34 ct total weight designed by Gelin and Abaci Inc. *Courtesy of www.weddingband.com.* Mounting only: $695.

Illusion

Settings can be designed to make a stone appear larger.

Illusion setting in a gold and solitaire diamond ring. *Courtesy of Robyn Stoltzfus.*

Multiple-stone Settings

The setting of multiple stones in one ring calls for different requirements. Some multiple-stone rings use solitaire settings for each stone, and other styles also have developed.

Bezel Settings

Bezel settings in an 18K gold, platinum, sapphire, and diamond ring, c.1900. *Courtesy James Robinson, NY, NY.*

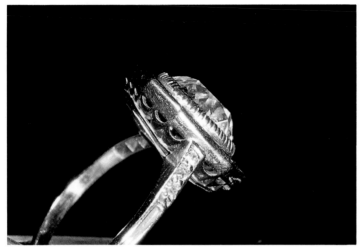

Bezel- set center stone surrounded by callibre stones, as seen from the side. *Courtesy James Robinson, NY, NY.*

American platinum, diamond, and sapphire ring with center marquise shape diamond approx. 1.27 ct **bezel-set**, callibre sapphires cut to fit the design, engraved shank, c.1920. *Courtesy James Robinson, NY, NY.* $12,000 - 14,400.

Channel Settings

Man's platinum and 18K gold wedding band with 4 **channel-set** diamonds of 0.50 ct total weight designed by Diana. *Courtesy of www.weddingband.co.* $3,015.

Cluster Settings

Above & left: **Cluster-set** ring with gold band and diamonds set in silver prongs, 19th century. *Courtesy James Robinson, NY, NY.*

78

American **cluster-set** yellow gold and diamond ring with large center diamond of fancy cinnamon color surrounded by ten white prong-set diamonds, c.1930. *Courtesy James Robinson, NY, NY.* $12,000 - 14,400.

American platinum, sapphire and diamond **cluster-set** ring with light color sapphire, c.1910. *Courtesy James Robinson, NY, NY.* $9,500 - 11,400.

American 18K gold, platinum, sapphire and diamond **cluster-set** ring with dark color blue sapphire, c.1910. *Courtesy James Robinson, NY, NY.* $9,850 - 11,820.

Edwardian 18K gold and platinum ring with center sapphire of medium color blue surrounded by **cluster-set** diamonds, English, c.1910. *Courtesy James Robinson, NY, NY.* $13,000 - 15,600.

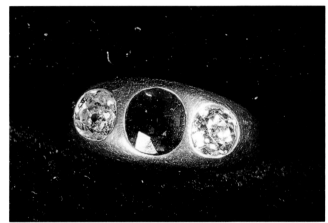

Gypsy setting.
Victorian 18K gold and
three diamond ring,
English, c.1900.
*Courtesy James
Robinson, NY, NY.*
$6,875 - 8,250.

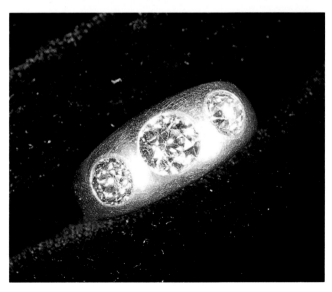

Gypsy setting.
Victorian 18K gold
three stone ring with
center diamond and
two side sapphires,
English, c.1900.
*Courtesy James
Robinson, NY, NY.*
$6,875 - 8,250.

80

Pave Settings

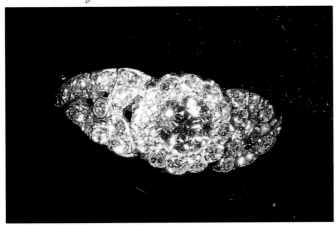

Pave setting. American platinum and diamond ring with cluster pave setting, c.1930. *Courtesy James Robinson, NY, NY.* $9,500 - 11,400.

Prongs

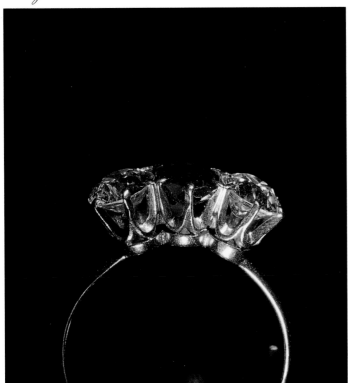

Three-stone ring with **prong setting** in gold, two round diamonds, and a ruby. *Private collection.*

Left: Platinum **prongs** on emerald cut diamonds with side mountings, American, c.1925. *Courtesy James Robinson, NY, NY.* $13,750 - 16,500.

Below: Three-stone ring with platinum **prong settings** for two emerald-cut diamonds and emerald on a gold band. *Private collection.*

82

American 14K gold, sapphire and diamond ring with a crossed **prong setting**, c.1880. *Courtesy James Robinson, NY, NY.* $8500 - 19,299.

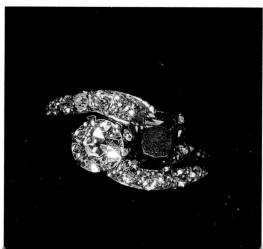

Custom Designing Your Engagement Ring

At some point in the search for your engagement ring, you may be inspired to create your own unique design, and you should be encouraged to explore this possibility. Not every jeweler you meet will be equipped to help you, especially if the jeweler does not have the equipment or trained staff to do the work. The cost, effort, time, and creative urge spent to design a unique engagement ring may be *more or less* than choosing a finished or easily available engagement ring, but only you know if those are limiting factors. You may be able to use family stones available to you in any setting you want to imagine. Or combine a variety of ideas to create your design. The possibilities are limitless and only you have to be satisfied.

Custom designing your engagement ring can be a happy, shared experience.

Ring Sets and Wedding Bands

Your search for an engagement ring may be accompanied by your thoughts about a wedding band. Some people choose to not have a wedding band, others choose to not have an engagement ring, and still others want both, accompanied perhaps by additional guard rings. We all have our unique reasons and impulses.

If you expect to choose both an engagement ring and a wedding band, their compatibility for the man and the woman alike can be a consideration. You may want them designed as a set, or you may want to combine one old and one new. Various wedding band designs are symbolic, such as twisted bands of contrasting metals or a metal band with a line of stones. Here your imagination and personality will lead your choices.

Ring Sets

Lady's 14K yellow, white, or rose gold mounting designed by Bagley & Hotchkiss. Mounting only: $490. Lady's 14K yellow, white, or rose gold wedding band by Bagley & Hotchkiss. *Courtesy of www.weddingband.com.* : $350.

Left: Lady's 18K yellow gold and enamel mounting available in blue, black, green, or red designed by Henry Design. *Courtesy of www.weddingband.com.* Mounting only: $300. **Right:** Matching lady's 18K yellow gold and enamel band also available in blue, black, green, or red designed by Henry Design. *Courtesy of www.weddingband.com.* $335.

Matching set of platinum and diamond rings with baguettes, c.1970. *Courtesy of Blair Loughrey.*

Left: Lady's platinum and diamond wedding band with 15 brilliants of 0.15 ct total weight designed by Elber-Rosenthal Ltd. *Courtesy of www.weddingband.com.* Mounting only: $ 1,155.
Right: Matching lady's platinum diamond mounting with 20 brilliants of 0.24 ct total weight designed by Elber-Rosenthal Ltd. *Courtesy of www.weddingband.com.* Mounting only: $ 2,890.

Left: Platinum engagement ring mounting with baguette diamonds of 0.75 ct total weight. Mounting only: $2,795.
Right: Platinum wedding band with baguette diamonds of 0.33 ct total weight, both rings designed by Diana. *Courtesy of www.weddingband.com..* Wedding band: $1,565.

Top: **Left:** 18K two-tone gold engagement ring mounting with 20 brilliant cut diamonds, 0.52 ct total weight designed by Jean-François Albert. Mounting only: $2325.
Right: 18K gold and diamond wedding band with 13 brilliant cut diamonds, 0.29 ct total weight designed by Jean-François Albert. *Courtesy of www.weddingband.com.* $1,220.

Center: **Left:** 14K gold and diamond mounting with 2 brilliant diamonds of 0.03 ct total weight designed by Folkways. *Courtesy of www.weddingband.com.* Mounting only: $865.
Right: Matching 14K gold and diamond wedding band with 3 brilliant diamonds of 0.04 ct total weight designed by Folkways. *Courtesy of www.weddingband.com.* Mounting only: $686.

Bottom: **Left:** Lady's 14K yellow gold and diamond mounting with 8 brilliants of 0.06 ct total weight designed by Henry Design. *Courtesy of www.weddingband.com.* Mounting only: $510.
Right: Matching 14K yellow gold wedding band with 20 brilliants of 0.18 ct total weight designed by Henry Design. *Courtesy of www.weddingband.com.* $630.

Left: **Claddaugh rings**: **Left:** 14K gold and diamond Claddaugh wedding band containing 5 brilliants of 0.10 ct total weight designed by The Celtic Collection. *Courtesy of www.weddingband.com.* Man's size: $294. Lady's size: $266.
Center: 14K yellow gold and diamond Claddaugh wedding band containing one brilliant of 1/7 ct tw, 13 mm at top tapering to 5 mm designed by The Celtic Collection. *Courtesy of www.weddingband.com.* Man's size: $364. Lady's size: $336.
Right: 14K yellow gold Claddaugh wedding band 12.5 mm at top tapering to 3.5 mm

designed by The Celtic Collection. *Courtesy of www.weddingband.com.* Man's size: $161. Lady's size: $137.

Right: **Left:** Man's 14K yellow gold wedding band with antique finish. **Center:** Lady's 14K yellow gold wedding band with antique finish. **Right:** Matching 14K yellow gold engagement ring, all designed by David P. Vertue. *Courtesy of www.weddingband.com.* Man's band: $298. Lady's band: $266. Engagement ring mounting only: $325.

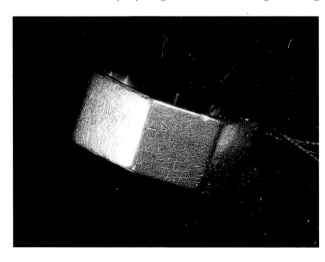

George V, three-color 18K gold band of geometric design, English, c.1930. *Courtesy James Robinson, NY, NY.* $1685 - 2,022.

87

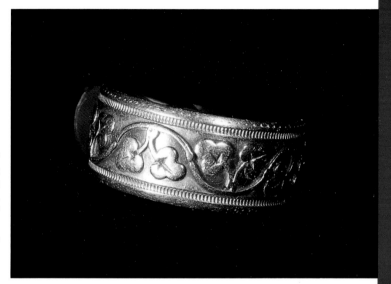

Victorian three color 18K gold band with ivy design made in Birmingham, England, in 1880. *Courtesy James Robinson, NY, NY.* $1,950 - 2,340.

14 K or 18K yellow, red and white gold, sterling silver and copper Mokume (wood grain metal) band with square or round edge designed by George Sawyer. *Courtesy of www.weddingband.com.* $750 to $1,210 depending on ring width, ring size, and metal combinations.

14K or 18K yellow, red and white gold, sterling silver and copper Mokume (wood grain metal) half round or flat band designed by George Sawyer. *Courtesy of www.weddingband.com.* $550 to $1430 depending on ring width, ring size, and metal combinations.

Platinum and 18K gold, 8.0 mm wide *Sekitei* wedding band with textured surface designed by Michael Bondanza. *Courtesy of www.weddingband.com.* $1,455.

Posy rings. Both of these rings are "posy rings," known to have love sentiments inscribed in Gothic around the band. *"Vous et nul autre,"* in French, means in English "you and no other." 14K yellow gold wedding band designed by Folk-ways. *Courtesy of www.weddingband.com.* Man's ring: $250. Lady's ring: $220.

14K yellow gold wedding bands designed by David P. Vertue. *Courtesy of www.weddingband.com.* Man's band: $335. Lady's band: $290.

14 K yellow gold wedding band, 3 mm wide, with West African Adinkra symbols designed for the Sankofa Collection by Kotto Awoowoo. *Courtesy of www.weddingband.com.* $425.

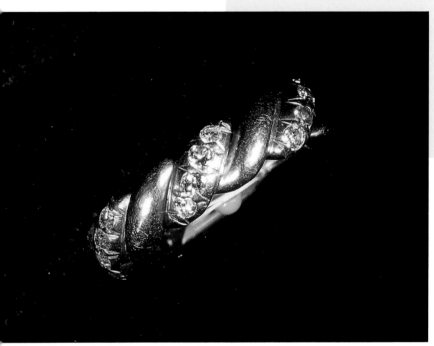

American 14K gold and platinum band twisted with a line of diamonds, c.1940. *Courtesy James Robinson, NY, NY.*

14K yellow gold wedding band, 7.5 mm wide, with West African Adinkra symbol of a cowrie shell which has been used to adorn royalty and nobility and been used as currency. Designed for the Sankofa Collection by Kotto Awoowoo. *Courtesy of www.weddingband.com.* $750.

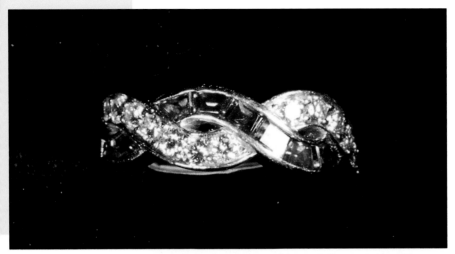

American platinum, sapphire and diamond ring with a
twisted band made by Wechter & Co. of Chicago, c.1940.
Courtesy James Robinson, NY, NY. $6,250 - 7,500.

Platinum, 24K and 18K gold
wedding band set with 6 brilliant
cut diamonds of 0.17 ct total
weight and 6 square cut sapphires
of 0.76 ct total weight designed by
Michael Bondanza. *Courtesy of
www.weddingband.com.* $2,890.

Ring guards. Lady's 18K
yellow gold and enamel
band available in blue, black,
green, or red designed by
Henry Design. *Courtesy of
www.weddingband.com.*
$200.

Anniversary band. Lady's platinum and diamond anniversary band with 6 baguettes and 8 brilliants of 1.05 ct total weight designed by Martin Flyer. *Courtesy of www.weddingband.com.* $2,520.

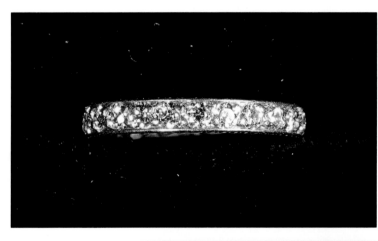

Eternity Band. Platinum and diamond eternity band made by Tiffany & Co., c.1920. *Courtesy James Robinson, NY, NY.* $5,750 - 6,900.

Eternity band. American platinum and diamond eternity band of white diamond baguettes, c.1930. *Courtesy James Robinson, NY, NY.* $4,500 - 5,400.

Bridal jewelry
including a diamond
tiara from Fred
Leighton, a diamond
engagement ring,
and diamond stud
earrings designed by
Hammerman.
*Courtesy of Diamond
Information Center.*
Photograph by Jim
Bastardo.

4 After You Choose Your Engagement Ring

If your heart has led the search for your engagement ring up to this point, it now the time for your head to do a little work to secure your selection.

Written Guarantees

Reputable jewelers can provide you with a written description of anything they sell and should offer you a receipted bill of sale on their letterhead stationery. Smart buyers will ask for a written guarantee for their purchase if it is not offered by the jeweler first, and no one needs to feel awkward at this important part of the selection process. Unless you, yourself, are qualified to determine the various factors that identify the ring you have chosen, you should obtain a warranty of its attributes.

The jeweler should verbally describe the style and components of your ring, while you take notes. Many jewelers can plot the flaws or identifying characteristics on a paper "map" showing the shape and facets of the stone. A written, dated, and signed guarantee should include a description of all the components and the current market value. Check your notes against the jeweler's statement to make sure they agree. You are just being intelligently cautious, not suspicious, by confirming your understanding of what you have chosen.

For diamonds over one carat in weight, and for many colored stones, you can and should ask for a Certificate of Authenticity from an accredited gem testing laboratory to accompany your ring. (See also Chapter 1, Identification Systems.) To obtain one, a reputable jeweler will send the ring, or just the stones if that is the case, away to the testing laboratory for analysis. Within a short time, the lab will return the gem/ring along with an official certificate stating the particular attributes. This document becomes a fingerprint of your ring and can be used for future reference.

The most well-known gem testing laboratories are:

American Gemological Laboratory (AGL)
580 Fifth Avenue 12th floor
New York, NY 10036

Gemological Institute of America (GIA)
Gem Trade Laboratory
580 Fifth Avenue
New York, NY 10036

Gemmological Association and Gem Testing Laboratory of Great
Britain
27 Greville Street
London EC1N 8SU England

Appraisals

No matter what style, value, or type of engagement ring you
have chosen, you can obtain an objective opinion about a ring's
composition and value by having it appraised by an independent
appraiser. Many people can sell jewelry, but only those who have
studied to become professional, accredited, jewelry appraisers are
qualified to make a judgment of your ring and will stake their
reputation on it in writing. A second opinion should always be
sought if you cannot adequately make the judgment yourself. The
fee required to have a ring independently appraised should be
included in your calculation of the cost of purchasing the ring. By
following this step, you can avoid any surprises and also confirm
your own knowledge of the ring.

Before you settle on the terms of payment for the ring, ask for
a reasonable time to have the ring inspected by a third-party appraiser either at the jeweler's location or at a place of your choosing.

Appraisers in your neighborhood can be found through various national trade associations such as the following:

Appraisers Association of American
60 East 42nd Street
New York, NY 10165
Telephone: 212-867-9775

American Society of Appraisers
Box 17265 Dulles International Airport
Washington, D.C. 20041
Telephone: 1-800-272-8258
website: www.appraisers.org

International Colored Gemstone Association
22643 Strathern Street
West Hills, CA 91304
Telephone: 818-716-0489

American Gem Society
5901 West 3rd Street
Los Angeles, CA 90036
Telephone: 213-936-4367

Accredited Gemologist Association
1615 South Foothill Drive
Salt Lake City, Utah 84108
Telephone: 801-581-9000

Canadian Gemological Assoc.
P.O. Box 1106, Station Q
Toronto, Ontario, Canada M4T 2P2

Jewelers of America, Inc.
1271 Avenue of the Americas
New York, NY 10020
Telephone: 212-489-0023

National Association of Jewelry Appraisers
4210 North Brown Avenue, Suite A
Scottsdale, AZ 85251
Telephone: 602-941-8088

Paying for the Ring

Most jewelers will be pleased to work out a comfortable payment schedule with you. Credit plans, interest payments, and installment plans may enable you to afford the ring you have chosen. Ask questions that will lead you to a successful method of payment.

Insurance

To protect yourself from the possibility of financial strain if your ring ever becomes damaged or lost, seeking an insurance program that covers personal property or specific jewelry may be a good idea. Usually, an insurance underwriter will require an official receipted bill of sale or recent appraisal of your ring to establish its current value before issuing you insurance protection.

Care of Your Ring

Caring for your ring properly should be your one of your first considerations after choosing your engagement ring. How do you take care of your ring so that it will give you the pleasure you expect from such an important piece of jewelry?

Cleaning

To maintain the pristine look of a new ring, or the continuing sparkle if it has gemstones, it should be cleaned once a month. Normal skin oils, cosmetics, soap, and grease can gradually build up to make a ring look dull. Different people may share their favorite method of cleaning their jewelry with you, but only you can decide to accept or decline these methods. The recommended methods here have worked well.

Ammonia and Cold Water

Soak the ring in a solution of half ammonia and half cold water for thirty minutes. Drain the extra solution off on paper, but do not rinse.

Liquid Detergent and Warm Water

Brush the ring with a solution of a mild liquid detergent dissolved in warm water, using a soft toothbrush or other soft brush. Place the ring in a wire strainer and rinse it under warm running water to remove the detergent and dirt. Dry carefully with a soft cloth.

Commercial Jewelry Dips

Several liquid jewelry cleaning solutions are available in the markets. Follow the instructions on the package.

Storage

When it is not being worn, your ring (and other jewelry) should be kept safely in **only one place**, a thoughtfully selected and softly lined container. By choosing **only one place**, you will not wonder where you put it later. Diamonds will scratch each other and other jewelry if they are thrown into a jumbled jewelry case or drawer.

As You Live With Your Ring

Each day you wear your ring, it becomes a source of pleasure because of its meanings, both personal and within your society. Common sense will enable you to live comfortably with it. A few extra reminders may be worth repeating.

Chlorine bleach can discolor and pit the metal in jewelry.

A hard knock can chip gems, including diamonds. Therefore, take your ring off when you do rough work, play sports, or even wash the dishes. Extra grease does it no good.

Have a jeweler, perhaps the one from whom you chose your ring, check your ring once a year to detect any damage, loose prongs, or heavy dirt build-up. Sharing the care of your ring with a trusted and experienced professional can add to your enjoyment of it.

5 *A 4-Step Guide to Making the Right Choice*

Step 1: Before you go to the jewelry store

Step 2: First visit to the jewelry store

Step 3: Learn for yourself, read the sections
that interest you in this book

Step 4: Second visit to the jewelry store

Step 1: Before you go to the jewelry store

Admit you have little or no experience buying an engagement ring.
Ask yourself: What am I looking for? What is my budget?

Read several advertising pieces in newspapers and general magazines **carefully**.
Notice what they show in pictures and say in words.
Make notes of the ads and store locations.
Discuss your findings and listen to your own questions and answers.
Make a list of your unanswered questions.

Choosing the stores to visit

Independent jewelers in your neighborhood may be convenient and realistic in their understanding of your needs. Ask relatives and friends for recommendations and their opinions of a jeweler's reputation.

General stores with jewelry departments that sell large volumes of jewelry, and rings in particular, include Sears and Penney's. In the United States, the highest carat volume of diamond sales takes place with Sears jewelry departments. These stores have plenty of reputation to guard and lots of experience to bring to your search.

Specialized chain jewelry stores with several locations can offer a variety of styles and volume sales. Often located at shopping malls where the highest volume of customers pass by, they combine volume with convenience.

International jewelers with designers of their own, such as Tiffany & Co, Cartier, Inc., Buccelati, etc. can offer fine quality and reputations with original designs.

Antique jewelry dealers can show you old and antique styles that are not available on the new jewelry market.

Step 2: First visit to a jewelry store

Before speaking with a sales person, get an overview of the type of jewelry that is for sale. Look around quietly by yourself. You can learn a lot by your own response to the personality of the store and your observations of the clients and store personnel. Perhaps visit several stores and look around each by yourself.

When you feel confident about your expectations and questions, and think the personnel are knowledgeable and stable (you will want to be able to find them again), engage a sales person in casual conversation. Let the sales person tell you generally about their jewelry. Keep control of the conversation yourself by stopping them if you begin to feel uncomfortable, rushed, or overwhelmed.

If you feel confident in the brief conversation with the sales person, ask them **ONE** of the questions on the list you made in Step 1. Listen carefully to the answer and think if it makes sense to you. They should be able to teach you enough so that you can understand the answer.

If you feel confused, thank them for their time and end the conversation. You may need to revise your question, or find someone else at a different store who can answer your question with more security.

When you feel comfortable with the answer to your first question, ask another from your list. For your future reference, ask for a business card of the person with whom you speak and take notes the information you want to remember. Try the rings on, or ask to see them on someone's hand. Rings can look very different on different size hands than they do alone in a jewelry case.

If you are considering having a ring custom designed, ask if this store can do the job for you. They may have designers who can help you make your ideas a reality, or they will let you know that they do not have these services. Many stores can only sell the items they have on inventory.

Repeat Step 2 at other stores until you feel completely comfortable with a sales person and the personality of a store and its merchandise.

Step 3: Learn for yourself

Read, look at, and talk about the information in the various sections of this book that interest you and have given you a basic knowledge about engagement rings. Different stones, metals, styles, traditions, and combinations exist or can be made to suit you as an individual. This knowledge may answer some of your initial questions and raise others.

Have conversations with respected professionals and trusted friends with experience buying an engagement ring.

Make and stick to your budget. Some people suggest that you should expect to pay two months' salary for an engagement ring. You can establish your top dollar figure so you establish the boundaries of your purchase.

Make a new list of questions you want answered.

Step 4: Second visit to a jewelry store

Now that you have a well-considered idea of your expectations and have basic knowledge to build upon, return to the sales person(s) with whom you have the most confidence. Ask a new question and listen carefully to the answer. Consider the answer in relation to your new deeper knowledge. If you feel confused by what you hear and see, thank the sales person for their time and end the conversation.

If you feel satisfied by the answer you have received, ask another question. This may prompt other, deeper questions and result in a real exchange of knowledge that helps you to be more confident in your expectations. Do not let the sales person talk you into something you have not thought carefully about. Keep control of the conversation by sticking to your written questions and make written notes about the answers.

When you (and your partner / fiancee) have satisfactory answers to all your questions, you may be ready to select an engagement ring that meets your expectations, price, and feelings. You are making an educated and confident decision. May your ring bring you great pleasure and years of happiness.

Bibliography

Chadour, Anna Beatriz. *Rings, The Alice and Louis Koch Collection, Forty Centuries seen by Four Generations*. Leeds: Maney, 1994.

Gemological Institute of America, *Colored Stones Course*. Santa Monica: Gemological Institute of America, 1980.

Matlins, Antoinette L., PG, and Antonio C. Bonanno, FGA, PG, ASA. *Jewelry & Gems, The Buying Guide, How to Buy Diamonds, Colored Gemstones, Pearls, Gold & Jewelry with Confidence and Knowledge*. Woodstock: GemStone Press, 1997.

Schiffer, Nancy N. *The Power of Jewelry*. West Chester: Schiffer Publishing, Ltd., 1988.

Wilde, Matthew. "World Diamond Congress Tackles Lasering." *Rapaport Diamond Report*, vol. 21, No. 30 (7 Aug 1998): 1.

Index

Accredited Gemologist Association 97
Adinkra symbols 89, 90
Albert, Jean-François 61, 86
alexandrite 48
alluvial deposits 12
American Gem Society 97
American Gemological Society (AGS) 34, 38, 42, 96
American Society of Appraisers 97
amethyst 49
anniversary band 92
antique rings 6
Appraisers Association of America 96
aquamarine 49
Art Nouveau style 8
ArtCarved 22, 27
Arts and Crafts style 9
Awoowoo, Kotto 89, 90

Bagley & Hotchkiss title page, 27, 30, 62, 84
baguette 25, 29, 30
baguette cut 23
Baguette World 62, 64
baroque pearl 57
Beaudouin 8
Bennett, Murrle & Co. 69

beryl 48
Bevaqua, J.A. 22
bezel facet 17
bezel setting 67-69, 75, 76
blister pearl 57, 58
Bondanza, Michael 89, 91
bridal jewelry 93
brilliance 15
brilliant cut baguette 32
brilliant cut 16, 17, 21, 23, 30-34
brilliants 22, 25
Buccelati 101

cabochon 46
cameo 9
Canadian Gemological Association 97
carat (ct) gemstone weight 40, 59
care 98, 99
Cartier, Inc. 28, 50, 101
caveties 38
Celtic Collection 87
Centenary Diamond 10
channel setting 77
chips 32
chrysoberyl 48
citrine 48, 49
Claddaugh rings 87

cleavage flaw 38
cluster setting 77-79
collet setting 67
colored stones 46-55
colorless crystal 38
Conway, Judith 33
Cooper, John Paul 9
corundum 51, 52
cowrie shell 90
Création Thibaudeau Inc. 61, 64
crown 17
cubic zirconia (CZ) 45
culet 17
cultured pearl 57
custom designing 83
cuts of diamonds 15-34
CZ (cubic zirconia) 45

dark spot flaw 38
DeBeers Collection 35
demantoid garnet 48
diamond color enhancement 36
diamond grading reports 42, 43
diamond clarity 27
diamond color 34-36
diamond imitations 45
diamond clarity enhancement 39
diamond clarity scale 38
diamond cutting 14, 16
diamonds 10-45
Diana, the Princess of Wales 52
Diana 60, 77, 85
Dixon, Stephem 33
dream cut 32

earrings 93
Elber-Rosenthal Ltd. 25, 29, 55, 64, 69, 85
emerald cut 23, 24, 29, 33
emerald 9, 48, 50, 82
enamel 8, 69, 91
engraved shank 73
engraving 6
eternity band 92
European cut 19
Evans, Judith 2, 3, 65

Faber, Aaron 33
Fabulite 45
facet 17
fancy color diamond 35, 36, 78
faulty cuts 18, 19
feather flaw 38
flaws 37, 38
fluorescence 35, 42
Flyer, Martin 4, 30, 92
Folkways 61, 86, 89
fracture filling 39

French pearl 57
freshwater pearl 57
Fusaro 63, 64, 65

gadolinium gallium garnet (GGG) 45
garnet 45, 48
Gaskin, Arthur and Georgie 9
Gelin and Abaci Inc. 33, 74
Gemmological Association of Great Britain
    96
Gemological Institute of America (GIA) 34,
    38, 42, 43, 47, 96
Gemprint 44
gemstone identification report 47
GGG (gadolinium gallium garnet) 45
girdle 17
girdle fringes 38
girdle roughness 38
glass 45
gold 8, 59-62
grain 57
graining flaw 38
gypsy setting 80

Hammerman 71, 93
heart cut 23
Henry Design 84, 86, 91

identification systems 44
illusion setting 75
inclusions 37, 38
Infinity Line 22, 55, 65
insurance 98
International Colored Gemstone Association
    97
irradiated diamonds 36

Jewelers of America, Inc. 97
Jwaneng Mine 11

karat (k) gold weight 40, 59
Kashmir blue (sapphire) 52
Kimberley Mine 13
Kind, S. & Son 55
knaat flaw 38
Knox, Archibald 6, 53

laser inscribed diamond 44
laser drilling 39
le Turcq, Georges 8
Leighton, Fred 93
Liberty & Co. 7, 53
loupe 5, 37

Mabé pearl 57
make 16
Mark Michael Designs 4, 29, 34

marquise cut 23-27, 33
melee 29, 34
Mexican opal 48
millegraine 6, 19, 69
Mokume 66, 88
morganite 48, 49
mother of pearl 49
multiple-stone settings 75-82
Myers, Rebecca 46, 65

Naper, Ella 9
National Association of Jewelry Appraisers 97
natural flaw 38
natural pearl 57
nick 38
Nielsen, Evald 8

old-mine cut 19
opal 7, 8, 48
openwork setting 73
oriental pearl 57
oval cut 23-25
Oved, Sah and Mosheh 66
oyster 57

pave setting 81
pavilion 17
Pavitt, William Thomas 48
pear cut 23-25
pearl 8, 9, 46, 49, 56-58, 67
peridot 48
pigeon's blood (ruby) 51
pinpoint flaw 38
pits 38
platinum 63-65
Pliny 50
points 40
posy ring 89
premier diamond 35
princess cut 32, 33
prong setting 70-72, 81, 81

radiant cut 32
rhinestones 45
rhodolite 49
ring guards 91
ring sets 84-86
rose cut 19
round cut 30, 33
rubellite 48
ruby 19, 48, 51, 52

Saint-Yves 56
Sankofa Collection 89, 90

sapphire 6, 45, 48, 49, 52-55, 75, 76, 79, 82, 91
Sawyer, George 66, 88
scarab 6
scratch 38
seed pearl 57
Sekitei 89
settings 59-93
shell 49
silver 66
single cut 32
Socrates 9
solitaire settings 67-75
South Africa 10
Spencer, Edward 9
spinel 45, 48, 49
spread 40
square cut 28
Stern, H. 33
swindled stones 20
synthetic diamonds 45
synthetic sapphire 45
synthetic spinel 45

table 17
table cut 19
Tacori 33, 63
tanzanite 49
tear-drop cut 24
tension setting 74
tiara 93
Tiffany & Co. 92, 101
topaz 48, 49
tourmaline 48, 49
traditions 6, 11, 50, 51, 54, 58
trilliant cut 32, 33
tsavorite garnet 48
turquoise 9
twin lines flaw 38

Vertue, David P. 87, 89
Vever Maison 8, 36
volcanic pipes 11

Watt, James Cromar 8
Wechter & Co. 91
wedding bands 87-91
Wellington Diamonds 45
Wilson, Henry 9
written guarantees 95

YAG (yttrium aluminum garnet) 45
yttrium aluminum garnet (YAG) 45

zircon 48, 49